France
today

France today

Introductory studies

Third edition

Edited by
J. E. Flower

Methuen & Co. ∽ London
Barnes & Noble Books · New York

First published 1971
Second edition 1973
Third edition revised and reset 1977
Published in Great Britain by
Methuen & Co Ltd
11 New Fetter Lane, London EC4P 4EE
and in the U.S.A. by Barnes & Noble Books
10 East 53rd Street
New York NY 10022
USA

© 1971, 1973 and 1977 Methuen & Co Ltd

Typeset by Red Lion Setters, Holborn, London
and printed in Great Britain by offset lithography
by Billing & Son, Guildford, London and Worcester

ISBN (Methuen) 0 416 85700 0
ISBN (Barnes & Noble) 0-06-472211-2

Contents

Foreword

While it is possible that this book may be considered by some to provide background material for literary studies and by others to encourage a comparative assessment of England and France today, these are not its main aims. It has been written instead to stand in its own right as a series of informed, up-to-date accounts and analyses of key aspects of modern-day French civilization. Some chapters — those on the church, the press and recent foreign policy, for example — contain material that is not readily available in English elsewhere except at considerable length and in greater detail; others, notably those on political parties and education, elucidate complex subjects by analysing them at least in part in a historical perspective, while Chapter 1 on French society supports the factual information it has to offer by a first-hand knowledge of some of the problems involved.

Contributors have been left free to deal with their subjects as they have thought best. Their views are based on research and careful analysis, and all have wide teaching experience in the field about which they have been invited to write. Each chapter closes with detailed suggests for further reading. It is hoped that these six essays will encourage students to turn to the more detailed works that have been recommended, not only with some prior knowledge of the issues at stake but above all with interest and enthusiasm.

John Flower
Norwich, May 1970

Note to the second edition

The principal difference between this second edition of *France today* and the first is the inclusion of a chapter on trade unions which provides a valuable and necessary extension to the opening sections on society and political parties. Readers already familiar with the 1971 publication will notice other changes which, we hope, are to the good. The majority of articles have been extensively rewritten; all have been brought as far up to date as printing schedules will allow and the bibliographies have been revised.

I should like to express my thanks to Charlotte Heman for her careful preparation of the Index for this edition.

John Flower
Norwich, January 1973

Note to the third edition

A major difference between this edition and the second is the essay by Alan Clark on foreign policy which replaces the chapter previously contributed by Maurice Keens-Soper. Once again readers to whom the earlier editions are familiar will notice that extensive rewriting has taken place particularly in the chapters which deal with the church and the press. Contributors have taken as many of the events of 1976 into account as has been possible and all bibliographies have been brought up-to-date.

John Flower
Exeter, October 1976

1 Social structures

Andrée Shepherd

Introduction

French society today can no longer be neatly divided into the traditional units of ruling class, middle class, working class and peasantry. During the last hundred years in particular wars and revolutionary movements, shifts of population and developments in industry, science and technology, have all helped to create a kind of uniformity and standardization which makes any clear-cut divisions of this nature difficult. This trend has also been emphasized by the changes that have occurred in the more traditional institutions of society — the church, the family, the educational system and even military service. Society is now very much on the move, a fact which has only been recognized fairly recently in a number of important changes — an attempt to break down excessive centralization and encourage the development of regions as more autonomous units, the spreading of social and cultural services and changes in social legislation. Inevitably the future is still uncertain; what is unquestionable is the wind of change.

Population

Today France has 52.6 million inhabitants including 4.2 million foreigners (1975 census), most of them immigrant workers from North Africa and Southern Europe. In spite of low birth and death rates and with immigration almost at a standstill since 1974, the population is still increasing but at a much slower rate of growth (+ 0.6 per cent per year compared to + 0.9 per cent in 1970). During the last thirty years French governments have decidedly been in favour of larger families — the *Code de la Famille* was first drafted in 1939 though not put into effect until after the Second World War — and more recently still there have been large-scale press campaigns to encourage French people to have more children. The government is introducing comprehensive measures in favour of families with a child under 3 or with three children at least, in an attempt to reverse the trend of a decreasing birth rate and of families with two rather than three children. The marriage rate is falling steadily (from 8.1 per 1000 in 1972 to 7.4 per 1000 in 1975) and the fertility rate has decreased even more dramatically: from 2.9 per woman in 1964 to 2.1 in 1974, and falling below replacement level in 1975 with a figure of 1.9. But in spite of a declining birth rate, 25 per cent of the population is still under 20. Consequently there is a working population of some 22 million with 30 million dependent on it and, with the proportion at work still decreasing owing to the lowering of the age of retirement and to the high level of unemployment, there is a mounting burden on social and educational services.

A large proportion of the population lives in towns — nearly 30 million in 1962, and 35 million in 1968 (compared with 17.5 million in 1911) — with the migration from countryside to town an ever-present and continuing trend. But what is more significant still is the fact that the population is becoming tripartite: 17 million in towns proper, 17 million in suburbs and *grandes banlieues* (expected to increase to 25 million in the next twenty years), and the remaining one-third spread over a countryside of about 500,000 km². This growing suburbia is creating new challenges and new problems. The architectural horror of Sarcelles near Pontoise, for example, brought with it fresh social problems. The very existence of this type of dormitory-suburb, catering for vast numbers of industrial and office workers, has had unexpected consequences, one of which, for example, is a growing tendency to introduce the continuous working day, which only ten years ago would have been anathema to French workers used to one- or two-hour lunch breaks. But the real solution may be elsewhere: developing these distant suburbs into viable economic units. From 1956 to 1965, Sarcelles grew from 8,400 to 30,000 inhabitants: a *grand ensemble* with no life of its own.

Socio-cultural facilities have gradually changed it into a proper town. Sarcelles 1972, with its 56,000 inhabitants, regional commercial centre, grammar and secondary schools, town library and cultural centre, industrial development zone and municipal bus service, no longer relies on Paris, although it is only some nine miles away. A few miles further north the new town of Cergy Pontoise is being built around new factories, office blocks and schools in an attempt to avoid previous mistakes, but with only mitigated results since, together with the other four New Towns in the Paris area, it suffers from its too rapid growth rate and its closeness to the capital.

As we might expect, internal population movements have meant a radical change in the distribution of people between the industrial and the agricultural parts of France. In 1962, 21 per cent of the active population was in agriculture (as against 45 per cent at the end of the nineteenth century), while 38.5 per cent was in industry. Over the last 15 years, the number of farms has decreased 30 per cent, and is still decreasing: in 1975 only 10 per cent of the active population was concerned with agriculture. But a direct comparison between industry and agriculture is not the most instructive from the point of view of the changing social structure of the country as a whole. More revealing is an examination of the distribution of the labour force between the primary sector (agriculture, forestry and fisheries), the secondary sector (mining and manufacturing industries, building, gas, electricity) and the tertiary sector ('non-productive' occupations, for example, social services, health and education). In 1962 the tertiary sector was already in the lead (41 per cent of the labour force) followed by the secondary (38 per cent) and the primary (21 per cent). In other words it is the non-productive sector which is larger than either of the other two. More interesting still is the recent trend which shows signs of a more profound transformation in society: a high rate of expansion of the tertiary sector (+ 11 per cent between 1962 and 1968, + 8 per cent between 1968 and 1972), a dramatic decrease of the primary (which lost 20 per cent of its share), and a slow progress of the secondary, mainly due to a short-lived boom in building and public works between 1962 and 1968.

In the tertiary sector, the professional classes and *cadres* alone have increased by almost one-third so that they now form some 10 per cent of the working population. A continuation of this trend because of further technological change, mechanization and rationalization may be expected to lead to a society in which only a minority will be directly involved in production, with the majority occupied in administrative and servicing activities. In such a situation there may be a number of consequences. On the one hand the division between manual and non-manual workers could become more marked, leading to a greater proletarianization of a smaller manual working class, and to an intensification of the class struggle. On the other hand, a large number of workers are facing redundancy, so that unless extensive retraining facilities are developed quickly, the wealth created by automation will heighten the problem of inequality and a new class of 'unemployables' will emerge.

Country v. town

France has often been described as a nation of small farmers; as F.C. Roe once put it, a 'garden in which millions of peasants dig, plough, hoe and weed from sunrise to sunset'. But these peasants are slowly being drawn in by the expanding towns, and in particular by the octopus-like metropolis. Some people consider that such depopulation of the countryside will lead inevitably to the general impoverishment of the rural communities left behind, others that the regrouping of land will create more economically viable units.

Generalizations of this nature are, of course, dangerous, because of extreme regional variety. The great plains of the Paris Basin with their rich crops of wheat and intensive farming, the mixed-crop farming of Brittany or the Rhône valley, the vine-growing areas and the mountain deserts of Central France present widely differing problems and prospects. The healthy areas seem to be of two kinds: the capitalist type of intensive farming; and the more traditional type of mixed farming, which, by increasingly involving co-operative enterprise, fulfils the need of modern agronomy for skilful crop rotation and division of labour. Future prospects are certainly favourable given certain assumptions: that there is a concentration on products in high demand (fruit, vegetables, high quality wine); sufficient organization (syndicates and co-operatives); well-planned marketing. In some favoured areas like the Côte d'Or, the agricultural labour force (vineyard labour) earns salaries comparable to those of the Dijon factories nearby. In less prosperous ones, like Brittany, however, some poultry farmers are worse off than industrial labourers. A large firm may deliver them day-old chicks and chicken food and impose precise planning. After nine weeks they collect the chickens for slaughtering. The farmer is a home-labourer paid to work according to conditions laid down by the firm. He may own his poultry farm, but this is probably a liability as he is usually tied down by debts of up to 20,000 F, and is entirely dependent on the firm employing him. Several poultry farmers have managed to organize themselves into a co-operative and are attempting to capture a greater share of the market, but this is an exception. For the majority proletarianization has reached the countryside in a brutal form, and even in the richer Rhône valley there are increasing tendencies for farmers to contract with freezing and canning firms, like the American firm Libby's. All too often the farmers' share in the profits is a minor one.

In the last fifteen years or so, a certain amount of government planning has been introduced in an attempt to improve the lot of many rural communities. Demonstration areas (*zones-témoins*) were created in 1952, but with only a small measure of success. Agricultural schools and training, almost non-existent under the Third Republic, have been developed. Since 1966, television has also been used, through the *Télé-Promotion-Rurale* educational programmes made by five regional centres. They cover two-thirds of the country areas and use group discussions and expert advice to tackle practical problems relating specifically to each area. Since 1973, government grants to the equivalent of two thousand pounds are being given to young farmers willing to settle in depopulated areas and loans for equipment are now easier to obtain.

More important perhaps for the future are the growth of tourism, which is bringing a new lease of life to areas often beautiful but deserted (the Massif Central and mountainous areas in general), and the allied popularity of 'week-end cottages', which is leading to the resuscitation of dead villages (again in the Massif Central and in Haute Provence) or the invigoration of depopulated ones. The development of the touristic potential of the mountain areas must be accompanied by greater training facilities for the new jobs, in hotels and catering for example, which allow more young 'barmen farmers' to stay in their village and earn a proper wage. There are also industries contracting out work (as did the Nottingham lace industry in the nineteenth century) over large areas of countryside. This *saupoudrage industriel* as it is called provides regular work for women at home or winter occupation for the whole family. This is the case with watch-making in the Jura, textiles in the Loire, footwear around Cholet (near Nantes) and cutlery in the Lozère, though it can and does lead frequently to the exploitation of cheap labour.

A fact of which an increasing proportion of the rural population is becoming bitterly aware is that, far from being protected by the welfare state, it has never received its full share of the national income while doing more than its fair share of work. By comparing his lot with that of people in other areas of France and in other countries, the French peasant has become more aware of his lower income for harder work and longer hours than town people and the lack of cultural facilities and modern conveniences. The growing unrest, very often among younger people, and in depressed areas, has led to a radicalization of the peasant movement over the last fifteen years and profound changes are in the making in the agricultural community.

It is traditional to underline the divorce between Paris and the provinces. Taine put it in a nutshell in 1863: 'There are two peoples in France, the provinces and Paris, the former dines, sleeps, yawns, listens; the latter thinks, dares, wakes and talks; the one dragged by the other like a snail by a butterfly, now amused now worried by the capriciousness and audacity of its leader.' As the focus of national life in France, Paris is unrivalled and the Parisian has a haughty attitude towards anybody who does not belong there. This is somewhat surprising to outside observers who happen to know that while one in every five Frenchmen lives in Paris or the Paris region, only a small proportion has been established in the capital for more than a generation. In spite of the pressure of life in the capital, the constant rush and noise, the desperate housing situation, and the very high cost of living, the prestige and desirability of life there were unaltered until very recently. Stifled by cars which encroach even on the pavements, much of the old Paris is being demolished and replaced by tall tower blocks. As a result, it is emptying itself of its original population which cannot afford the cost of renting or purchasing the luxury flats which are replacing the old and too often insanitary buildings. There is now a move towards the outskirts of the city, or even quieter provincial centres, an expansion that has recently been acknowledged by the administrative reshuffling of the whole Paris area, which had become unmanageable.

Just as it is a social centre, so, too, is Paris an intellectual one: with its thirteen university campuses, and its flood of students it is in great contrast with quieter provincial university towns. But is prestige necessarily matched by excellence? It may be, since there is severe competition for both teachers and students. Paris is the place where teachers, as indeed most civil servants, aim to end up before retirement: a visible way of measuring their success. Paris used also to be considered the world's cultural capital. It is still a very lively but expensive centre; many of the new films can now be seen in provincial towns for one-third the price of an *exclusivité* in the Champs-Elysées or the Boulevards, while the decentralization policy for arts (music, theatre, visual arts) and the increasing number of summer festivals have made culture available to more provincials than ever before.

With industry the situation is similar and in spite of efforts to decentralize the town is bursting at the seams. Tax rebates are awarded to industries moving outside the Paris area, but these do not seem to have made much impression since the general underdevelopment of the provinces (communications in particular are poor) counteracts government incentives. While Paris itself, with its 2.3 million inhabitants, lost 11.1 per cent of its population between 1968 and 1975, the greatest increases in population were in the other areas of the Paris conurbation which includes the five New Towns of the metropolitan area.

Recent years have also seen the fostering of provincial conurbations to serve as poles of attraction, such as the Rhône-Alpes region, with the already enormous Lyon complex (well over 1 million inhabitants) and much publicized expansion of the Winter Olympics town of Grenoble. Only four towns have 500,000 (Lyon, Marseille, Lille, Bordeaux); another nine have over 300,000. Compared to the 9.8 million inhabitants of the Paris conurbation, this shows a lack of balance greater than in Britain.

Efforts to fight the growing suffocation of Paris have been extended by a policy of regionalism, which is still causing a great deal of controversy. Regionalism is a positive effort to adapt to the requirements of contemporary life and needs. It involves the formation of viable and autonomous economic units, rather than a negative rejection of the arbitrary division into *départements* and a resulting return to historical provinces. The ninety departments have thus been grouped into twenty-one economic regions, the eight of the largest towns have been singled out as *métropoles d'équilibre*. But real administrative and industrial decentralization is proving difficult. Too many Paris-based firms are setting up one or even several factories in the provinces while retaining their '*Siège Social'* in Paris. As a result, decisions are taken in Paris without enough direct knowledge of local conditions. Recently the government has been advocating a more diversified system of regional development: in the provinces, the development of both the *métropoles d'équilibre* and of the *villes moyennes* (50,000 to 80,000 inhabitants), helped by better rail and road communications between towns and more specialization of each industrial centre to avoid costly competition within one region. However, the *question régionale* still remains, with its political, economic and cultural undertones: it will be used in political and electoral manoeuvring. The economic under-development of certain areas (Brittany, the Landes, the Massif Central) and the redeployment of labour will disrupt existing social groupings and nationalist, political or religious minorities will act as pressure groups and attempt to restructure the whole surrounding community. An encouraging sign is the recent reversal of the trend in migration from the Brittany and Loire valley rural areas.

Family and youth

Recent population changes have meant an increase in the

number of families with two rather than three children: the answers to population surveys on ideal family size give an average of 2.58 children per family in 1974 by comparison with 2.88 in 1947. While single-child families are undoubtedly becoming rarer, the low percentage of very large families remains constant. Economic conditions have, of course, a determining influence on the structure and evolution of the family. The introduction of family allowances is only one of the measures of the *Code de la Famille* aimed at relieving the financial burden of bringing up children; there are also, besides the family allowances proper, allowances to a single wage-earner (*allocations de salaire unique*), prenatal and maternity allowances, housing, and child-minding allowances. To these, a special allowance for single mothers is to be added (October 1976) — an attempt to counteract the supposed effects of the Abortion Act (1975). Quite clearly, these are government incentives to encourage the average French family to have three children or more, and more comprehensive measures are announced. Yet other factors, like poor housing, future educational and professional prospects, the desire to retain a high standard of living, and the availability of contraception (1974 Act) and abortion — though with more restrictions than in England — tend to have the opposite effect.

This is where differences appear between young parents and the previous generation. There is no longer a willingness to have larger families at the expense of a standard of living painfully attained through the added source of income of the increasingly numerous working wives and mothers. This in itself creates new problems: that of the younger children, for whom there are crèches and nursery schools in large towns and industrial areas in much greater numbers than in England; the health of the mother and her personal attitudes to her husband, children and work (the working mother's feeling of guilt seems to be more strongly ingrained in Britain than in France); and the problem of the ultimate stability of the family as a basic unit of the social structure (statistics show that marriage is still a stable institution and that in spite of strains and tensions, only one in ten marriages ends in divorce, though the 1975 Divorce Act may initially cause a sharp increase in the figures). Young couples seem more flexible, more able to adapt their attitudes to the necessity of the working mother than were their own parents (who reached parenthood during or immediately after the war, and hence in special circumstances and difficulties). There is less of an inward-looking, obsessively maternal attitude, and instead a more 'liberal' outlook towards child-rearing, which no doubt will bring its own set of problems when today's children reach adolescence.

However, some traditional elements remain, though these are less marked in large cities than in smaller communities. Everywhere, close ties still exist between the small family unit (parents and children), and the extended family (grandparents, uncles, cousins, and so on), ties which have survived the move of the children to the city. Parental authority, respect and politeness are on the whole more sternly enforced than in England, though all this is being eroded in urban communities. In this respect, France seems nearer to Irish than to English customs, though just how far this is due to a common Roman Catholic tradition is difficult to ascertain. Traditional values are certainly more firmly upheld in rural communities like the Pays Basque or Vendée, where traditions die hard.

In the early sixties, the cult of youth invaded advertising, fashion and the entertainment and holiday industries. And *les jeunes* were the basis of France's faith in its political and economic future. This faith was shaken by the explosion of May 1968 when suddenly young workers and students were seen as a threat to the establishment. Until then the rebellious minorities had largely been ignored by the wider public. Even pop culture was tame; it was the reign of *les copains* walking hand in hand and listening to Johnny Halliday on their transistor radios: nothing resembling the wild English or American crowds. They were on the whole conforming to accepted patterns of behaviour. The more culturally aware formed the audience for Georges Brassens, Juliette Gréco and other upholders of the poetical or political tradition of the *chansons*; the more politically minded were militant in innocuous-looking *groupuscules* torn by in-fighting.

Rebellious youth has been brought to the fore since May 1968 — untamed university and secondary school students, unorganized union militants — all defying the establishment.

They have questioned authority in all its manifestations and have won some concessions. The student wave seems now to have receded, although protest will be simmering under the surface as long as educational reforms are not properly implemented, and this will take years, thousands of new teachers and millions of francs. As the youth wave of the early sixties reaches adulthood and enters a labour market shaken by the unemployment crisis, the adult world reacts with hostility and fear. Today, in some areas of Northern France, 60 per cent of the unemployed are under 25, most of them women. In spite of special efforts made by the *Agence Nationale de l'emploi* (National Labour Exchange), half a million of them need more than three months to find their first job, and 16 per cent of those registered are still unemployed after a year. Whether they have just left technical school, grammar school or University, they are faced with the same problem: too few openings. Whether or not they are politically committed or have now withdrawn into conformity, they are not 'opters out'. A great deal of fuss is made over drug-taking, but this is much less of a problem than in Britain. One reason may be that in a more competitive system, French children enjoy a less liberal education than their British counterparts; if they take a stand against it, they rebel — which is a positive even if threatening reaction.

Social classes

The traditional condition of the working class has changed considerably in the last fifty years. The growth of unionization, the system of social security and the increased mechanization of industry leading to an overall higher level of training and specialization, have certainly led to a higher standard of living for a large number of workers. Some problems remain, others are heightened. There is in particular a sense of insecurity at a time when many industries are under threat: mining, as in Britain, is declining; the car industry is shaken by regular crises; even in more advanced sectors like the aircraft industry, rationalization and mergers have led to redundancies on a large scale.

The improvement in the standard of living by comparison with pre-war conditions is a misleading way of appreciating the real situation. There is an ever-widening gap between the very rich and the very poor. The growth of wages has not kept pace with the cost of living and the expectations of a society which seeks to improve itself materially and consumes more. There are also new cultural and leisure 'needs' as the shortening of the working week slowly spreads, though time thus gained is often wasted commuting to more distant suburbs.

What is emerging however is a new sub-proletariat, concentrated on the outskirts of large conurbations, especially Paris, and largely consisting of untrained immigrants. There are over 4 million of these, mainly from North Africa. They live in overcrowded shacks (*bidonvilles*) and lodging houses, and although many treat them as foreign outcasts, they are a necessary, though often thought undesirable, part of the labour force. Some attempts have been made by local councils to integrate them, by offering families council flats in HLM (*Habitations à Loyers Modérés*), even though there is often quite strong resistance to this by local French residents.

While the average working-class standard of living may approach that of the pre-war middle class, such a change is much less marked in France than in England (house ownership is far less common, although the family car and, more recently than in England, the television set, are becoming part of working-class life); and class consciousness seems to have remained sharper. It may be due in part to the 25 per cent of communist voters who, while not being a 'revolutionary' force, still keep alive a certain language or jargon and an analysis based on the class struggle; it may be due also to a labour movement, which has not, as in England, been torn apart to the same extent by the compromises of participation in government.

At the other end of the social scale, the wealthy *grande bourgeoisie* still possesses considerable power and influence, particularly in the Chambre des Députés (the legislative) and in the administration (the civil service, parts of which, like the Foreign Office, are open only to members of the *grande bourgeoisie* or aristocracy). Its economic rule is, of course, undisputed, though the frequency of mergers, and take-overs by foreign firms, cause signs of strain to appear. In the educational, social and cultural spheres, it has fared less well.

State education, anti-clerical and fairly democratic (but perhaps more a formal than a real democracy), has almost completely escaped its grasp and become a threat and open adversary, in that it educates a youth that will stand against the interests and principles upheld by the *grande bourgeoisie*. But one must here distinguish between the *lycées classiques* (grammar schools), *modernes* (secondary schools) and *techniques* (technical schools) which though they all in theory cater for anybody according to ability do in fact have a different *clientèle*. The *lycées classiques* are still largely a preserve of the bourgeoisie, while the others, because of geographical distribution and lack of prestige, get more working-class and fewer brighter children. However, the unification of syllabuses, the *tronc commun* for all the children between 11 and 15, and centrally organized examinations, though criticized for being overdone, are helping to standardize things.

The new extended middle classes are not a purely French phenomenon. But there are some specific French characteristics: the number of minor civil servants (*petits fonctionnaires*), who often earn less than manual workers, do a repetitive and often tiring type of office work, and yet consider their position as a promotion, mainly on account of the 'image' (white-collar worker) and the security (no fear of redundancy and a guaranteed retirement pension) that such posts offer.

It must be recalled here that the French civil service includes, besides administrative workers, other sections of the working population like teachers and post-office workers, and the social status of teachers is certainly higher than it is in Britain, through large numbers of supply teachers (a quarter of the total number) have low pay and no security of employment. Teachers are generally held to belong to the very French category of *cadres*, which forms a new middle class largely corresponding to the growth of the tertiary sector. The *cadres* are distinguished from managers because they are salaried workers, not employers. They may be responsible for a large section of a factory or administration (*cadres supérieurs*) or only a smaller group of workers (*cadres moyens*). The *cadre supérieur* earns on average four times as much as a worker. In some industries, they represent 3 per cent of the salaried workers (mining), in others 12 per cent (mechanical and chemical industries), even 18 per cent (power) or 19 per cent (oil). They enjoy a high standard of living, due to the relative security of their jobs; but they too are increasingly suffering from unemployment and inflation. Their number has been estimated at around 1 million, and it is still rising. They mainly enjoy a better education, are more numerous in large towns and differ from the traditional bourgeoisie by their more reckless way of life with a lower tendency to save, and greater tendency to consume.

What is happening, therefore, is more a blurring of the visible signs of class distinctions than a destruction of class barriers themselves. Some categories are desperately clinging to the past: small shopkeepers, older farmers, small industrial enterprises. But most people want to join the 'civilization of plenty', the 'consumer society', and families who used to spend a high proportion of their income on food seem to give higher priority to such things as household appliances, cars, television sets or holidays. The search for security is a key word for the working classes, now favouring the monthly paid status to the hourly paid insecurity of the past. Secure employment can only guarantee them the maintenance of a newly acquired higher standard of living, which is also threatened at present.

Of the unifying elements between the social classes, some are fast changing. Conscription, for example, is still enforced, and young men face twelve months of military service. Until the Second World War this period *sous le drapeaux* used to create a real melting pot, some kind of initiation rite in which young men from varying backgrounds shared. It still remains a meeting ground, but offers much less social mixing. Great numbers of students used to obtain several years' delay, but the 1970 law is trying to enforce early military service for all young men of eighteen, and attempting to bring down from 33 per cent to 18 per cent the proportion of exemptions from military service. However, students still tend to serve their time as teachers in ex-colonial countries or, if they serve in the armed forces, very often do so as NCOs, and in any case do not mix well because of their age and different interests. So the rift between educated and uneducated, young and poor, is no longer bridged as it once was by this common experience of army life. Conscription itself provokes bitter controversy.

Other common factors remain, though. A good many French children have, at some time in their childhood, spent a holiday in a *colonie de vacances* where children of unskilled labourers rub shoulders with children from higher social backgrounds. Like the state education system, this type of holiday camp must have some levelling influence, since money is not the criterion for admission: the social security system partly provides for those parents who cannot afford the cost of their children's holidays spent in this way. In the field of recreation and holidays, there is one major change in the habits of the French; families did not normally go away on holiday together, below a comfortable income level, unless they were visiting relatives still living in the country. With the extension and lengthening of paid holidays (four weeks for all now, and in some cases a calendar month), there is a noticeable increase in the number of French families going camping, or even caravanning, in the summer. The French seem obsessively to live for *les vacances*, a magic word: half the population regularly migrates in the summer, while farmers account for nearly half of those who remain behind. Holidays no longer are the privilege of the rich. The spectacular success of such institutions as the Club Méditerranée, with its thatched-hut villages around the Mediterranean, as well as in more exotic places like Tahiti, is a witness to this change. Even skiing holidays, still a preserve of the upper middle class (only 4 per cent of the population can afford them), are in a minor way open to the underprivileged, through the system of *classes de neige* whereby primary schools from town areas can in turn send one or more classes to the mountains for a month, complete with teacher and skiing equipment, to combine normal teaching in the morning with outdoor activities in the afternoon. This is still far too sporadic for it to be effective in any general way, and too expensive for all children concerned to be able to go, but it does point to a future when more of what was the privilege of the better-off could be available to many more.

Society on the move

In May 1968, after ten years of stable Gaullist rule, France woke up in turmoil. The country came to a standstill, the regime itself was threatened. Everything seemed to be questioned: parliament and political parties, trade union bureaucracies, the educational system, the mass media, bourgeois culture. Indeed France has not been quite the same since. But it would be wrong to ascribe the continuing muta- tions of French society to these 'events' — they have simply sharpened some aspects already in existence.

Organizations. Some organizations, like trade unions, under- line the class struggle, while others, like political parties and the church, tend to cut across class borders.

The church aims at being classless. It is true that the membership of the Catholic Church is drawn from all social classes, but while the Catholic hierarchy and the bourgeoisie are often linked, other tendencies of the church are associated with particular groups (for example, the worker-priests with the labour movement and the left-wing intellectuals); and its tolerance has sometimes proved to be a mixed blessing as when the JAC (*Jeunesse Agricole Chrétienne*) turned from organiz- ing Bible groups to militant action. In areas where the church is strong, it certainly serves to bind local communities together.

Political parties, despite the absence of any formal commitments, still tend to be associated with particular social classes or groupings — like the Communist Party and the working class, the UDR and the middle classes, the left-wing socialist PSU (*Parti Socialiste Unifié*) and the intellectuals or the Trotskyite *Ligue Communiste* and the students. These, like all generalizations, show only tendencies, not absolute truths; and in any case, all parties try to broaden their support. The general disaffection from traditional political parties, which was particularly clear in 1968, seems to be giving way to a new trend. While to some extent the 'majority parties' are joining forces around President Giscard d'Estaing with the approaching 1978 general election, there has been, as municipal election results early in 1977 showed, a marked increase in support for the 'united left' (socialist and communist parties) which with its Common Programme appeals to a broad cross section of the population.

Whether they are employed in the public or private sector, French workers are allowed to join trade unions, and this includes civil servants and senior staff. Compared to Britain, the number of workers in trade unions is low: no more than 25 per cent, though it fluctuates widely. But this is not the main difference. More important is the traditional and formal split between unions and party politics; trade unions always refuse to support a political party officially and there is no French equivalent to the Labour Party's financial support by union levy.

The main trade union confederations all have federations in the various professional and industrial branches: the communist led CGT (*Confédération Générale du Travail*), the CGT/FO (*Confédération Générale du Travail/Force Ouvrière*, which split from the CGT in 1947), and the CFDT (*Confédération Française et Démocratique du Travail*). The FEN (*Fédération de l'Éducation Nationale*) covers the majority of teachers, and the CGC (*Confédération Générale des Cadres*) is the main representative body of the *cadres*.

Union action welds workers together in the class struggle — the best recent example is the general strike of May-June 1968. But militant trade unionists are a minority of the workers, and the commitment of workers to their unions seems to be changing: the very militant are probably becoming more politically conscious and active, while the fringe only snatches a limited amount of time and energy from its main commitment to better living.

Recently there have been tensions between the rank and file and the union bureaucracies, with a dramatic increase in the number of unofficial strikes (*grèves sauvages*). Another recent trend is the ever greater importance given to claims for workers' control of the production and organization of work (*autogestion*) over traditional wage claims, especially in the CFDT. Both the CGT and the CFDT are pressing for a monthly minimum salary of 2000F (the SMIG now stands at 1500F), and for the lowering of the age of retirement for all.

Rural revolution. 'The silent revolution of the peasants', a phrase coined by Michel Debatisse, describes real, deep-seated changes in the rural community with the rise of his generation, which has started questioning basic traditional assumptions like land ownership. This new generation of farmers grew out of the Catholic organization, the JAC, which was formerly controlled by the local clergy and confined its activities largely to Bible meetings and socials. When they reached 25, the JACists usually left to get married, start a family and, unless they rented one, waited for their father (or grandfather) to pass on to them control of the family farm. After the war, the character of the JAC started to change considerably. Young militants began to put the emphasis on the need to provide themselves with professional training (accountancy and farming techniques) through study groups, and on gaining the culture of which they had been deprived by their lack of formal schooling and by the absence of cultural facilities.

By the middle 1950s, the JACists around Michel Debatisse decided to take steps and openly enter the trade union arena. The main farmers' union, the FNSEA (*Fédération Nationale des Syndicats d'Exploitants Agricoles*), was controlled by the older, richer, conservative farmers. But its moribund youth section, the CNJA (*Centre National des Jeunes Agriculteurs*) could be revived. They took it over and have gradually captured key posts in the trade union movement, while using their position as a platform for advocating new policies. They claim that peasant unity is myth, that there are rich and poor farmers whose interests are different. They admit that the rural exodus is normal — most of the existing small family farms are not economically viable — but they want it to be 'humanized' by the provision of proper training facilities. They do not deny the importance of maintaining prices, but wish to give precedence to structural reforms (land and marketing). Finally they question the sacred principles of property ownership and individualism: 'The fishermen do not own the sea. Why do we need to own the land?' They have started implementing their proposals by renting rather than owning their farms, by setting up group enterprises for marketing and shared production, by supporting the government agency set up for buying land and letting it in order to prevent speculation and by encouraging the regrouping of land (parcelled as a result of the equal inheritance laws dating back to Napoleon). The movement has not always been peaceful, however, and there were famous riots in Brittany in 1961, for example, when ballot boxes were burned. Michel Debatisse defines their overall aim well:

La propriété est-elle indispensable au métier d'agriculteur? Ce qui compte essentiellement, pour le paysan, c'est la sécurité. Hier, propriété était synonyme de sécurité. Demain, la notion de sécurité s'inscrira dans d'autres perspectives: statut du fermage renforcé, allocations familiales, dimensions plus importantes des exploitations, enseignement mieux adapté. A la propriété, il fallait substituer la notion d'un statut social de l'agriculture.

Michel Debatisse himself has now joined the ranks of the 'parent' organization, while the *Jeunes Agriculteurs* have found younger more militant leadership. Constant campaigning of the government has been effective; greater concentration and specialization has also had some benefit. Already, for example, because of the favourable Common Market tariffs, the emphasis is on cereal production rather than raising livestock, and large cereal producers are making huge profits, thus being able to enlarge further and invest; the old style co-operatives, in order to survive, have to federate into vast units and modernize their methods, while to be profitable the raising of livestock must be undertaken on a large scale. Not all have benefited however. Many farmers are crippled by debts and agricultural workers are among those with the lowest standard of living in the country. Rural life is thus rapidly changing beyond recognition.

Towards a cultural revolution? It is generally acknowledged that it takes three generations for the gradual change from the worker/peasant class to post-graduate or professional status to be achieved. But formal education, which plays such an important role in this, is not always attainable. The best *lycées* are not evenly distributed geographically, though this does not affect town-dwellers as much as country-dwellers; and the grants available for schoolchildren and students are scarce, and in most cases insufficient to ensure reasonable chances of success. These inequalities should be remedied in the long run, with the introduction of the *tronc commun* (common syllabus to all children starting their secondary education at the age of 11, whatever type of school they attend) and the possible introduction of some kind of *allocation d'études* to all students (which has been discussed by various political parties and student movements).

However, formal education at present is insufficient. Education must be a continuous process, and the alienation of the industrial worker — alienation of work on a machine, of closed community with no access to any culture, lack of time and facilities, poverty of mass media, etc. — causes him to revert to what one such worker calls illiteracy when he compares the reading and writing abilities of adult factory workers to that of their children still in junior schools (*Un ouvrier parle*, Enquiry by J. Minces, Paris, Seuil, 1969, pp. 54-7).

Although some basic conditions have been created for the deprived to have access to some form of education and culture, this may be less a reality than a pious dream. The expression 'Cultural Revolution' has, of course, got other overtones, but it is used here to cover the expansion of culture to an ever-growing audience by educating the public at large, thus creating an awareness of cultural needs, demands for cultural facilities, rejection of censorship and so on. One of the consequences of such an increased awareness would necessarily be the decentralization of culture, which is still largely concentrated in Paris and the more important towns.

In May-June 1968, with the breakdown of normal communications — press, radio, television — came what has been called an explosion of the word — everybody talking to everybody, in university lecture theatres and cafés and on the streets (this was of course, more true of large towns than villages, of Paris than the provinces, of young people than of old). For a short while, there was an impression of liberation from the constraints of normal life, an awakening, for people normally held down by routine. Theatre companies, journalists, writers, television personalities who visited the occupied factories and universities, were struck by the overwhelming response of their audiences. People became aware of the censorship of the government-controlled radio and television, of the cultural desert in which they were kept. But romanticizing is of no avail: the wave of excitement was followed by what may appear to be a return to the old state of affairs. When the striking ORTF journalists were sacked in the course of the summer of 1968, too few protesting voices were heard. The ORTF has a third television channel and is now split into seven rival companies. But censorship and government control, though unofficial, remain.

If there has been no *measurable* change, a new consciousness does exist, however diffuse. The dialogue between young and old may not have advanced much (not even in the trade union movement), and the multitude of news-sheets may be anarchic, but consumer groups are sprouting everywhere, organizing protest, putting pressure on civil service and local authorities. The barrier of communication must somehow have been shaken, especially among the young. Even in the *lycées* discipline and syllabuses have been transformed, and the schools are more open to the outside world. The introduction of 'participation', regretted by some as reformist, nevertheless reflects a change of attitude: disagreement only exists as to its degree and importance.

Decentralization of culture. There are 1200 *Maisons des Jeunes et de la Culture* (Youth and Culture Centres) in France, with some 600,000 members (half workers, half students and schoolchildren). They are subsidized partly by the state, partly by local councils, and administered by a permanent head (the large majority of whom have experience outside the educational profession) and a House Council elected by the young members themselves. Very often they are the only meeting-place for young people in small towns, apart from the local café, and are used for amateur dramatics, film shows, lectures, concerts, dances, and other indoor leisure activities; they also serve as a base from which to organize outings, holidays and so on. A high proportion of their worker members are active trade unionists, and their members in general are among the most literate apart from the students. Recently they have been under attack for being hotbeds of politicization of youth, and for wasting public money through bad administration. Both charges have been denied, but action has been taken against them. Under the pretext of decentralization, state subsidies have been reduced by 13 per cent, and more financial responsibility placed on local councils, who thus become direct employers of the staff. The consequences of this are tighter control over cultural policy by the local councils (generally right of centre) and a tendency to demand that what is supposed to be a public service should also be economically viable. Especially in the case of theatre, the development of a real cultural policy is increasingly being inhibited by the need to make a profit.

In 1951 Jean Villar became director of the *Théâtre National Populaire*; Roger Planchon gathered together his company in Lyon in the early 1950s; Jean Dasté's company was already successful in St Etienne; Jean-Louis Barrault was finally given the *Odéon Théâtre de France* in 1959 (only to lose it in summer 1968 as a result of the 'events'). In the provinces, the various *Centres Dramatiques* sprang up: the *Comédie de l'Est* (Strasbourg), *de l'Ouest* (Rennes), *du Centre* (Bourges), and so on. In the Paris suburbs there is a similar tendency to decentralization with the rise of the *Théâtre de l'Est Parisien* and others. The policy of these centres is to serve both the town where they are based and the surrounding rural community by regular tours. Their 'consecration' comes when they are invited to Paris for a season. Their aim is obviously to reach out to a working-class audience, and they partly succeed: some 30 per cent of the audience of Planchon's *Théâtre de Villeurbanne* is *populaire*. But the public reached is mainly skilled workers, foremen and the like, perhaps because the ordinary workers have fewer contacts with the trade union bureaucracy that handles the bookings. There is now an increasing realization that the theatre must go out to people in their normal surroundings; the problems then are how to combine artistic quality with mobility, and to determine what degree of effort can be demanded of the audience. Much more specific is the financial problem. The whole policy of decentralization, which gained such importance under the ministry of André Malraux, is in danger through lack of government support. Declarations by Edmond Michelet, when he was Minister of Culture, infuriated even the most moderate of directors, who were shocked, for example, by the remark he made in a television interview that 'the best theatre thrives on lack of money'. Only 0.4 per cent of the national budget goes to supporting the arts. The TNP was in dire financial straits after Vilar left it to Georges Wilson in 1963. It finally closed down in the summer of 1972, and Planchon's theatre was given the title of *Théâtre National Populaire*: another example of decentralization, but also the disappearance of the stronghold of popular theatre in élitist Paris. And provincial companies are constantly having to fight for survival because of lack of sufficient support from both government and local councils.

For a while the dream of a popular culture cutting across

class borders looked like coming true. At the moment, it seems greatly compromised. The gap between the culturally deprived (rural communities and the working class) and the cultured (Paris and the large towns, the educated middle classes) seems likely to remain for quite a long time.

Bibliography

Ardagh, J., *The New France* (revised edition). Harmondsworth, Penguin Books, 1970. A very comprehensive study, with precise examples. See Chapters IV, on farmers; VI, on provincial life; IX, on daily life; X, on youth, as the most relevant to social structure.

Beaujour, M. and Ehrmann, J. (eds.), *La France contemporaine*. New York and London, Macmillan, 1965. A collection of interviews and short articles covering all aspects of social, cultural and political life.

Bernard, P., *Le grand tournant des communes de France*. Paris, Colin, Collection U, 1969. Deals in particular with local government and provincial problems.

CERM (Centre d'Etudes et de Recherches Marxistes), *Les femmes aujourd'hui, demain*. Paris, Editions Sociales, 1975. Papers delivered by communist and non-communist thinkers and militants and the following debates. A very comprehensive survey of the condition of women today.

Debatisse, M., *La Révolution silencieuse. Le combat des paysans*. Paris, Calmann Lévy, 1963. A description of the movement of the young farmers by their leader.

Données Sociales, INSEE (Institute National de la Statistique et des Etudes Economiques) Paris, 1974. Statistical information on all aspects of social life, with an analysis of the main trends and reports on social surveys and consumer studies.

Dossiers et Documents, Paris, *Le Monde*, ten issues per year. A supplement to the well-known daily newspaper, gathering together recent articles concerning social, political and economic problems. A very useful tool for the student who wants to keep up-to-date with the evolution of French society.

Dupeux, G., *La Société française* (1789-1970). Paris, Colin, Collection U, 1972, and London, Methuen, 1976. See its analysis of the population structure and migrations in particular.

Esprit, L'Administration (Numéro Spécial). Paris, January 1970. On the administrative machine and the life conditions of the civil servant, an important collection of essays.

—, *L'Armée et la Défense* (Numéro Spécial). Paris, October 1975. In particular B. Kitou's inside view as a conscript, and the analysis of the 'malaise de l'Armée'.

Gachon, L., *La vie rurale en France*. Paris, PUF, Collection 'Que sais-je?', 1967. See pp. 100-24: 'The great mutation', the changes in rural life in the twentieth century.

Hamon, L. (ed.), *Les nouveaux comportements politiques de la classe ouvrière*. Paris, PUF, 1962. See the article by A. Détraz: 'Consommation ouvrière et attitude politique', pp. 248-52.

Hoffman, S. and others, *France: change and tradition*. London, Gollancz, 1963. See the article by L. Wylie, 'Social change at the grass roots'.

Lenoir, R., *Les Exclus*. Paris, Seuil, 1973. On the poor, the old, the handicapped, and all those who never gained entry to the consumer society.

Mallet, S., *La nouvelle class ouvrière*. Paris, Seuil, 1963. On the changes in working-class life and consciousness. English translation published by Spokesman Books, Nottingham, 1976.

Minces, J., *Un Ouvrier parle*. Paris, Seuil, 1969. Two long interviews with a working-class militant, before and after May 1968, describing the cultural alienation of a worker and formulating new, 'qualitative' demands. See in particular pp. 53-63 and 80-4.

Minces, J., *Les Travailleurs étrangers en France*. Paris, Seuil, 1973. A survey on the living and working conditions of immigrant workers.

Peterson, W.C., *The Welfare State in France*. Lincoln, Nebr., University of Nebraska Press, 1960. See Chapters II, 'The French Social Security System', and IV, 'The Distribution of Income in France'.

La Vie Catholique published in October 1972 the results of a large-scale enquiry (130,000 answers) on relations within the family, authority and freedom, marriage and sexuality, family and religion. Partial, but interesting.

Wright. G., *Rural Revolution in France*. California and London, Stanford University Press and Oxford University

Press, 1964. See its description of the new generation of peasants and its growing influence in peasant organizations, pp. 143-82, and 'Six village sketches', pp. 185-208.

2 Political parties

Eric Cahm

Introduction

The foreigner arriving in France during an election campaign could be excused for being mystified by the complexities of the party system. On every hoarding, a mass of posters, bearing a variety of sets of initials and slogans, exhorts the citizen to vote for any one of a dozen or more parties. Some of these parties, certainly, will be old familiar faces: the radicals, who go back to 1901, or the communists, dating from 1920. Others will be newcomers that have sprung into existence only since the last election. New parties are constantly being set up in France, each with its own set of initials, while old ones split down the middle, or simply take on a new name.

French party politics are thus both a complex and unstable, at any rate on the surface. The party spectrum never remains quite the same from one election to the next. How then does the average French voter find his way through this shifting kaleidoscope of names and abbreviations, which may denote not only single parties, but alliances between parties like the *Union de la Gauche* and the *Réformateurs*?

The basis of party divisions

Majority and opposition. He has, essentially, two sets of clues, two criteria to guide him. In the first place, since 1958, French parties have been readily classifiable at any point in time according to whether they are currently in the Gaullist majority in Parliament (*la majorité*) or are part of the opposition (*l'opposition*). The backbone of the majority has naturally been the party of the orthodox Gaullists, known at first as the UNR (*Union pour la Nouvelle République*), and now called RPR (*Rassemblement pour la République*). This was the party of De Gaulle's supporters, of Pompidou, Michel Debré, Chaban-Delmas, Messmer and Chirac; it championed and defended the Gaullist régime, and within that régime, played the leading role in state and government until the election of M. Giscard d'Estaing to the presidency in 1974. The *Républicains Indépendants*, M. Giscard d'Estaing's own original formation, have also been in the majority since 1962; they have expressed modest reservations about the régime. The MRP (*Mouvement Républicain Populaire*), representing Christian democracy, hovered on the brink of the majority until 1962, when it went into opposition. In 1966, Jean Lecanuet emerged as leader, and the group, still in opposition, was renamed *Centre Démocrate* — only to be renamed again as *Progrès et Démocratie Moderne* (PDM) by 1969! Meanwhile some members broke away under Jacques Duhamel to join the majority under the name of *Centre Démocratie et Progrès* (CDP). However, by 1974, the *Centre Démocrate* itself went over to supporting M. Giscard d'Estaing in the presidential election, and joined the majority after the election. The two halves of the party now finding themselves in the majority, it was natural that by 1976 they should join up again: the reunited group, led by M. Lecanuet, is called *Centre des Démocrates Sociaux* (CDS).

The leading party of the opposition is the Communist Party (*Parti Communiste Français* or PCF), led by Georges Marchais. Traditionally a revolutionary party, it has now finally thrown overboard the last vestiges of its old Leninist theory of revolutionary violence and committed itself to a total acceptance of parliamentary methods and the verdict of the electorate.

Its main partner in opposition, now that the former Christian Democrat formations of the Centre have both joined the majority, is the democratic socialist *Parti Socialiste* (PS), led by François Mitterrand. The *Parti Communiste Français* and *Parti Socialiste* have been allied since 1972 on the basis of a joint governmental programme, the *programme commun*. The Radical Party, taken over by the dynamic Jean-Jacques Servan-Schreiber in 1969, oscillated wildly under his leadership between moves towards the *Parti Socialiste* and moves towards Lecanuet's *Centre Démocrate*, ending up in October 1971 by joining Lecanuet in a movement called the *Mouvement Réformateur*. This alliance so riled some of the radicals under Maurice Faure that they broke away from Servan-Schreiber in June 1972 and offered their support to the communists and socialists. The opposition alliance, made up of the Communist Party, the *Parti Socialiste*, and these left-wing radicals (*radicaux de gauche*) now led by Robert Fabre is known as the *Union de la Gauche*. The remainder of the Radicals of the Jean-Jacques Servan-Schreiber variety supported M. Giscard d'Estaing in the 1974 presidential campaign, then joined the majority after his success. M. Gabriel Péronnet replaced M. Jean-Jacques Servan-Schreiber as Radical leader in 1975. Apart from the communists, socialists and left-wing radicals, the opposition also includes the PSU (*Parti Socialiste Unifié*), a small party led until late 1974 by Michel Rocard, and since by Michel Moussel, and, finally, the revolutionary extra-parliamentary opposition, dating from May 1968, with which the PSU is in close sympathy. This extra-parliamentary opposition is made up of splinter groups representing three main tendencies: Maoist, Trotskyist and anarchist. A more moderate extra-parliamentary grouping is made up of the *Groupes d'action municipale* (GAM), wedded to local action on civil issues.

Left, Right and Centre. The distinction between majority and opposition parties tells the voter something vital about each one, but is obviously not enough to distinguish fully between those on either side of the great divide. He tends instinctively, therefore, to apply a further criterion, and to distinguish parties into those of the Left, Right and Centre. Thus, though they are loath to admit it — no party in France will ever admit to being on the Right — the UDR and the *Républicains Indépendants* today make up the parliamentary Right. The communists, socialists and dissident radicals make up the Left, while the PSU and the extra-parliamentary opposition form the extreme Left. The Centre is made up of those formations sandwiched in the party spectrum between Left and Right: the *Centre des Démocrates Sociaux* of Lecanuet and M. Péronnet's

Radicals. Thus the line of demarcation between majority and opposition runs today between Centre and Left. The majority is made up in 1977 of the Right and Centre, and the opposition of the Left and the Extreme Left (see diagram, overleaf).

But what is the real meaning of these terms 'Left', 'Right' and 'Centre' to the French voter? These categories, unlike the endlessly shifting and short-lived party labels, have existed for a century and a half, and though there is a tendency at times to be sceptical about their meaningfulness, they are in constant daily use in the press and in conversation, and most of the time everyone really knows what they mean. They provide the handiest way of expressing, in shorthand form, the position of any party or individual politician, in relation to the rest of the political spectrum. While the programme of a man of the Left in 1977 obviously has a different content from that of a man of the Left in 1937 or 1837, he still differs from a man of the Right in 1977 in a recognizably similar way.

For and against the French Revolution. Originally, in the nineteenth century, the men of the Left got their name because they sat to the left of the President in French parliamentary assemblies; the men of the Right were those sitting to his right. This initial distinction between Left and Right reflected a difference of opinion about the French Revolution, and to this day the difference in political attitudes between left-wingers, who broadly support the principles of the 1789 Revolution, and right-wingers, who reject them, still forms the ultimate basis of the distinction between the two. Even in 1966, a radical spokesman did not hesitate to refer to the party's determination to 'donner force et vigueur aux conquêtes de la Révolution'. Left has thus continued to imply support for the French Revolution, Right to mean rejection of it. Throughout the nineteenth century, the men of the Left continued to believe, with the Revolution, that all men were born free and equal, both as regards rights in society and political rights. No king, no individual or group, they held, could claim by birth any social privilege, any absolute right to govern others; all political power stemmed from the people alone, and any popular government must take the form of a republic based on universal suffrage. Likewise, the authority

	L'OPPOSITION				LA MAJORITÉ			
	L'extrême gauche	*La Gauche*			*Le Centre*		*La Droite*	
	Revolutionaries	Communists	Democratic Socialists	Radicals	Radicals	Ex-Christian Democrats	Conservative Republicans	Orthodox Gaullists
	PSU (led by: Michel Moussel) *Ligue Communiste Révolutionnaire* (led by: Krivine-Trotskyists)	*Parti Communiste Francais* (led by: Marchais)	*Parti Socialiste* (led by: Mitterrand)	*Les radicaux de gauche* (led by: Robert Fabre)	*Parti Radical* (led by: Gabriel Péronnet)	*Centre des Démocrates Sociaux* (led by: Jean Lecanuet)	*Républicains Indépendants* (led by: Michel Poniatowski)	UDR (led by: Jacques Chirac)
		L'Union de la Gauche						
	Anarchists							
	Maoists							

of the Catholic Church in state and society was an affront to individual freedom and must be destroyed by the separation of church and state and the abolition of Catholic education. The Right, on the other hand, remained monarchist, believing in the need for authority in church, state and society, which could be reasserted by a return, if this were possible, to the system of the *Ancien Régime*, based on absolute monarchy, a social structure dominated by a privileged upper class minority and a Catholic Church enjoying a religious monopoly and unchallenged control over men's minds.

By the beginning of the twentieth century, the principles of the Left had apparently triumphed: universal suffrage had come to stay in 1848, the monarchy had been permanently replaced by a republic in 1875, non-religious state education had been introduced in the early 1880s, and the church was separated from the state in 1905.

However, Left and Right continued to represent conflicting viewpoints regarding the issues raised by the 1789 Revolution, which were not yet closed, despite all the progress which had been made towards putting the ideas of the Revolution into effect. Men of the Left stood not only for the defence of the new republican institutions, they could still look forward to the further extension of republican ideas in the direction of popular control of government and a more wholly secular society. Men of the Right could still look back nostalgically towards a society in which men deferred to authority, whether of politicians, bankers or priests, and could still try to ensure that, despite the coming of the Republic and universal suffrage, French society would remain firmly under the control of a superior minority rather than the mass of the voters. As for the religious issue, it had still not lost its power to divide Frenchmen by the time of the Fourth Republic, and indeed still flickers on to the present day, as the communist-socialist joint programme threatens the nationalization of church schools in the pursuit of secular principles (*la laïcité*).

In so far as men of the Right still look favourably on authority in politics, in the shape of the strong President introduced under the Fifth Republic, and still support a continuing role for the Catholic Church in French education, while men of the Left look for more individual liberty, more control of government by the voter, and moves away from church schools, the old meanings of Left and Right still, to a certain degree, hold good.

So, in the same way, does the traditional significance of the Centre as a position halfway between the two. For the Centre emerged in the nineteenth century precisely as a standpoint intermediate between that of the men of the Revolution and their opponents. And the importance of that Centre can be judged from the fact that the Right, before 1958, only enjoyed power during the decade preceding the Revolution of 1830, and in the Vichy period under Marshal Pétain. The Left has only held office for even more limited periods: during the short republican episode heralded by the 1848 Revolution and ended by the Napoleonic *coup d'état* of 1851; at the time of the Popular Front (1936-8); and at the Liberation (1944-6). It was, in fact, the Centre that in one form or another dominated French politics from 1814 to the beginnings of the Fifth Republic. The Centre and its policies can be seen, initially, as a form of compromise between the *Ancien Régime* and the Revolution. In their parliamentary form, the ideals of the Centre were defined in the *Charte constitutionnelle* of 1814, reintroduced with only marginal changes in the *Charte* of 1830. The concept of the restored monarchy was essential to the men of the Centre, known as liberals or Orleanists from their loyalty to the Orleanist branch of the royal family represented by Louis-Philippe. The monarchy was now, however, to be limited, not absolute. On the other hand, the powers of the people, too, were to be limited by the system of a restricted franchise. It was Guizot who declared that 'le suffrage universel n'aura jamais son jour'. In the religious sphere, the men of the Centre sought a compromise between the old domination of France by Catholicism and the secularizing zeal of the Left. Freedom of conscience was maintained, and in the *Charte* of 1814 Catholicism, which in 1801 had been recognized as 'la religion de la majorité des Français', was, though still a state religion, reduced to the status of one among a number of Christian sects enjoying equal state protection and subsidy. It was these ideas of the Centre which, in a modified form, continued to dominate French politics in the late nineteenth and twentieth centuries, as she was governed, under the Third and Fourth Republics, by a succession of governments based on the Centre. The parliamentary system allowed for a President, it is true, to occupy the monarch's old position as head of state, but the powers of the President were severely limited, for fear he should turn into an absolute monarch again; and, while the system was now based on universal suffrage, the actual political influence of the voters in any election was in practice largely nullified, as the deputies made and unmade governments within the charmed circle of Parliament, without regard to election results. The compromise still remained between absolute government from above and real popular control of government from below, while the control of French education continued to remain partly in the hands of the Catholic Church.

It is worth adding that Bonapartism appears at first sight to have been a movement of the Centre, transcending the distinction between Left and Right. The regimes of the First and Second Empires attempted, while paying lip-service to the Revolution and the rule of universal suffrage, to freeze the deadlock between the forces of the *Ancien Régime* and the Revolution which had set in by the beginning of the nineteenth century. The method of Bonapartism was to superimpose on this deadlock plebiscitary and authoritarian institutions, whereby the dictator derived his powers directly from the electorate as a whole, over the heads of the warring factions of Left and Right. Here, universal suffrage was distorted to cancel out the forces of Left and Right and sanction the dictatorial rule of an individual. It can easily be seen that despite the initial gesture towards popular control of government, and the Centre-based appeal to the nation as a whole, Bonapartism, like its successor Gaullism, really belongs on the right, since it involves effective concentration of political authority in the hands of one individual. And of course Bonapartism and Gaullism have both been favourable to the claims of the Catholic Church.

Labour against capital. Since the late nineteenth century, the basically political and social nature of the distinction between Left, Right and Centre has been overlaid, to an increasing extent, by a newer economic factor — the struggle between labour and capital — giving the Left a socialist and the Right

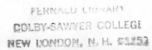

a capitalist flavour. In the twentieth century, therefore, the French voter has been able to distinguish left-wing parties, which have been in favour of socialism, from right-wing ones, which have clung to capitalism and free enterprise. Centre parties have here again stood for a compromise, involving not the abolition but the modification of capitalism — for example, through giving workers a share in management, profits or capital.

The twentieth-century party spectrum

The Left and socialism. In the nineteenth century, socialism arose out of the conflict between the owners of capital and those who owned nothing but their labour power, a conflict that had been heralded by Marx (and de Tocqueville at the time of the 1848 Revolution. While this conflict was all-too-apparent in the bloody clashes between workers and bourgeoisie in the June days of 1848, the idea of a political movement aiming at socialism, and based purely on the working class, did not become current in France until 1880.

Socialism remained for long simply a special feature of the extreme Left, inseparable from republicanism: under the Second Empire, the Paris workers remained faithful, for the most part, to the republican opposition. Even after the coming of the Republic in 1875, the workers continued to give their support to the radicals, who had become the most advanced of the republicans.

The socialists aimed, from the 1880s, however, at independent political action by a party of the working class. They aimed first at the capture of political power. This would be followed by the introduction of socialism, achieved through the handing over to society at large of the ownership of the means of production. Now the economic issue between labour and capital was made central for the first time to a political programme. For the republicans, economic changes had always remained very secondary to political and anticlerical measures.

French socialism was, from the outset, internally divided. The revolutionary Marxist socialists, who formed the *Parti Ouvrier Français* under Jules Guesde, held initially that the objectives of socialism — the capture of political power and the introduction of a new economic system — could be attained at one blow by a working-class insurrection. These revolutionary socialists regarded all struggles other than that of the working class against the bourgeoisie as irrelevant to the attainment of socialism. The traditional left-wing struggle for democracy and secularization was, therefore, of no concern to the workers. The democratic Republic itself was no more than an instrument for the class domination of the bourgeoisie. While Parliament might be a useful platform for propaganda, there must be no alliances with bourgeois parties and no participation in bourgeois governments. The socialist party must concentrate on its tasks of recruitment and propaganda among the workers in preparation for a revolutionary seizure of political power, to be followed by the expropriation of the bourgeoisie. Bourgeois democracy would rapidly wither away, and the workers would be in a position to usher in a classless society. The anticipation of modern communist ideas here is, of course, striking.

The reformist wing of French socialism, whose ideas were finally crystallized by Jean Jaurès, believed for their part in the attainment of socialism by democratic means. Hence the term democratic socialists, applied to them and to their successors in the twentieth century. They perceived a gradual movement towards socialism already taking place within bourgeois society. Unlike their revolutionary counterparts, they accepted the usefulness to the working class of the democratic Republic, parliamentary processes and even partial reforms within bourgeois society, such as the reduction of hours of work in industry.

They were prepared to ally themselves with the radicals, and even, with hesitation, to enter bourgeois governments. Alexandre Millerand was the first to do this, in 1899. At the end of the development within bourgeois society towards socialism, a final, decisive transformation of the property system would take place. The introduction of socialism could be brought about democratically, since, in view of the continuous growth of the proletariat, there would eventually be a majority in the country in favour of the social revolution.

By the end of the nineteenth century, socialism had thus joined radicalism on the Left, displacing it towards the Centre in the process. The more conservative republicans, for their part, had already moved into the Centre. These rightward movements form part of a frequently described process in the history of the French parties: beginning in opposition on the Left, they eventually gain power, carry out their programme, and then settle down to defend their achievement, both against the men of the Right, who would like to go back to the *Ancien Régime*, and against new men of the Left, clamouring for further reforms. The republicans went through this process after 1880; the radicals and the democratic socialists have gone the same way in the twentieth century.

At the beginning of the present century, the basic party divisions in France were beginning, as a result of the changes just described, to fall broadly speaking into the pattern which was to be characteristic of the whole period up to 1958.

The twentieth-century Left, properly so called, was to be made up of the two wings, revolutionary and reformist, of the socialist movement. The Socialist Party enjoyed a period of uneasy unity from 1905 to 1920, then divided irrevocably at the Tours Congress of 1920. The revolutionary wing now set up the French Communist Party, which was soon turned by Moscow into a faithful agency for the interests of international communism, as Moscow saw them. The old objective of the attainment of socialism by revolution remained, distant though this might often seem, and the party's organization, centralized and authoritarian, became the strongest of any party in France.

The reformists, or democratic socialists of the SFIO, were rebuilt into an effective party by Léon Blum after the 1920 split, attaining power for a time in the Popular Front period, when Blum himself became prime minister.

The Centre. The last two decades in the nineteenth century had seen the decline of the old monarchist and Bonapartist Right and Centre, a move into the Centre by the right-wing republicans, known as *opportunistes*, and the emergence of the radicals as the newest representatives of the republican Left. However, as we have seen, radicalism itself was being displaced towards the Centre by a new force, socialism.

The twentieth-century Centre included a number of parties. Traditionally considered left wing because of their strong anti-clericalism, the radicals formed themselves into a party in

1901, came to power in 1902, and were responsible, as members of the left-wing *Bloc des Gauches*, for measures against the religious orders, and for the separation of church and state (1905). It was at this point that, having achieved all their old programme, they moved into the Centre, becoming a party of the *status quo*, ready to defend the Republic against the Right, but wary of any substantial social changes. They became, in the twentieth century, so completely identified with the political system of the Third Republic that they described their party as 'l'expression même de la démocratie française'. Their position in the political Centre was brought out clearly by their views on the issue of socialism. While remaining, in principle, attached to the idea of private property, they were prepared to envisage measures of social welfare such as old age pensions. But they were more hesitant on such reforms than the socialists.

The conservative republicans equally belonged, at first, to the Centre. Descended from the old *opportunistes*, they formed two branches in the twentieth century. Their left wing consisted of the *Alliance démocratique*, founded by Waldeck-Rousseau in 1901, which remained faithful to the alliance with the radicals and to the ideas of the Centre, namely preservation of the political and religious *status quo* after the separation of 1905, and the maintenance of the rights of private property. Their right wing formed itself into the *Fédération Républicaine* in 1903, which looked for a more authoritarian Republic, remained attached to economic liberalism, and aimed at a rather nationalistic foreign policy. With the gradual abandonment by this group of its anticlericalism, followed by a re-assertion of Christian values, conservative republicanism completed its shift to the Right after 1945. The conservative republicans had been discredited during the war, but in 1954 they set up the *Centre National des Indépendants*.

After the First World War the Christian democrats emerged politically as a consequence of the gradual renunciation by a small number of Catholics of their old hostility towards the Republic and democracy. The small inter-war Christian Democratic Party, founded in 1924, was known as the *Parti Démocrate Populaire*. Its insistence on the rights of church schools led commentators to place it on the Right, on the traditional religious criterion. On the other hand, its economic ideas were more progressive than those of the radicals. By the time the Second World War and the Occupation had engulfed France, the Christian Democrats had evolved somewhat nearer socialism and the Left. Their ideas were based on the conception of democracy, which they sought to extend from Parliament to industry, and on the ideal of cooperation between capital and labour. At the Liberation, the Christian Democratic MRP took its place among French parties, rivalling the communists and socialists in the first years of the Fourth Republic.

The Right and free enterprise. Right-wing ideas first reappeared in the twentieth century in a violent form: the nationalism of the extreme Right. This extreme Right was largely the creation of the Dreyfus Affair. With the virtual disappearance of the old monarchist Right and Centre, national defence against the German threat took over from a restoration as the chief rallying cry of the Right. Since Dreyfus had been accused of betraying military secrets to Germany, the extreme Right, at the beginning of the twentieth century, seized the opportunity to claim that it was the spineless republican regime that was ultimately to blame. Maurras and Barrès looked for a firmer, more authoritarian political system, which could support more vigorous diplomatic and military measures against Germany. 'C'est une vérité générale', Maurras remarked, 'que la politique extérieure est interdite à notre Etat républicain.' Under the threat of a German attack, which became ever more real to many Frenchmen after the Kaiser landed in Tangier in 1905, the nationalist ideas of the extreme Right revived in the years before 1914, and brought with them a revival of the classic themes of counter-revolution: reverence for tradition and authority in state and society and, in the case of Maurras, the idea of monarchism itself. Right-wing organization has always been loose in France, and the anti-republican Right centred on Maurras's newspaper, the *Action Française*, which became a daily in 1908. Street agitation was carried on by the young bloods of the *Camelots du Roi*. This tradition of anti-republican agitation was carried into the more or less Fascist Leagues of the 1930s, which organized massive anti-parliamentary demonstrations on

6 February 1934, and were only banned when the left-wing Popular Front came to power in 1936.

More moderate right-wing ideas were seen in the republican Right, which, as has been noted, grew up in the twentieth century as the most conservative of the republicans completed their return to the ideas of the past, political authoritarianism and Catholicism, and espoused the defence of the interests of the small farmer and businessman.

Traditionalist ideas of the Right were able to stage a temporary come-back under the regime of Marshal Pétain in 1940. And, while De Gaulle defied Pétain in 1940, in founding the Gaullist Resistance he was reviving the essentially right-wing Bonapartist tradition, aiming at authoritarian government from the Centre, on the basis of a movement embracing the forces of both Left and Right on a national platform. The Gaullist movement dates from De Gaulle's London broadcast of 18 June 1940, in which he called on all Frenchmen to unite round him in resistance to Germany. Because of France's continuing divisions, De Gaulle was able, at least in times of crisis like 1940, 1947 and 1958, to create a broad national movement, which he saw as an expression of the will of the whole French people. Gaullism claimed to transcend existing party divisions, which were seen as harmful to France, and the General, standing above the parties, sought to draw his power directly from the people. There is in Gaullist doctrine an amalgam of ideas of Centre and Right. The notion that the head of state should be elected democratically by the whole people has a centre flavour, as have the other schemes, for profit-sharing and workers' participation in industry, proposed by left-wing Gaullists; on the other hand, Gaullism's insistence on a strong executive and an independent foreign and military policy for France are authoritarian and nationalist, and are more suggestive of right-wing principles. Despite the appeal to the Left, the main emphasis remains more right wing than centrist, and the practice of Gaullism is essentially authoritarian.

The Second World War and after

The party divisions of pre-1939 France, which, as we have seen, largely took shape in the very first years of the twentieth century, appeared to have been considerably transformed at the Liberation in 1944. The conservative republican and right-wing groups, though not all had collaborated with the Germans, seemed compromised with Vichy. The radicals had become discredited with the old Third Republic, of which they had always been the main champions. The Second World War and the German occupation had set off a massive left-wing reaction: socialism was in the air, and the communists and socialists shared a virtual monopoly of French political life with the now substantial MRP until 1947. This three-party period was dominated by the issues of post-war reconstruction, and by the introduction by the Left and the MRP of measures of nationalization, economic planning and social welfare. General De Gaulle saw no place for himself in the reviving party structure and resigned at the beginning of 1946.

It was only with the coming of the Cold War and the halting of social reform that the party system began to fall back into a more traditional pattern. From 1947, the threat to France from international communism seemed to overshadow somewhat the traditional threat from Germany. The Communist Party, being identified with the external menace emanating from Moscow, could no longer be tolerated as a governing party: it went into permanent opposition, breathing fire and flames against 'bourgeois' democracy, which it now denounced as a tool of American imperialism. Its period of identification with the French struggle against fascism, and even with the republican idea was ended. It reverted to its old revolutionary language, which had been put into cold storage during the Popular Front period, and throughout the period since 1941, when Stalin threw world communism into the struggle against Hitler. The French communists once again laid emphasis on their long-term theoretical aim, a violent seizure of power by the workers, to usher in socialism via the dictatorship of the proletariat. In the short term, they distorted the political system in two ways: since the communist deputies were permanently in opposition, all government majorities had to be formed by parties to *their* right, thus narrowing the margin of manoeuvre in Parliament for the other parties; and the party sterilized thereby the votes of a large section of the working class, who voted for the communists as the most 'progressive' party.

The other left-wing group, the Socialist Party or SFIO, began to move towards the Centre, chiefly under the impact of the Cold War. It came to accept as permanent the political and economic *status quo* of the Fourth Republic, which it sought to defend against communism and Gaullism. It began to give up, in practice if not in theory, its belief in the ultimate objective of socialism, and some saw it, indeed, as a new party of government — a sure sign of movement towards the Centre. The MRP, despite its own movement towards the Right, lost ground and met a serious setback in the election of 1951.

At the same time, the older parties of the Centre and Right reappeared on the scene. The radicals staged a come-back as the political habits of the Third Republic once more took over and the constitution of the Fourth Republic came to seem more and more like a carbon copy of that of the Third. Even the conservative republicans emerged once again, to set up, at the parliamentary level at first, the *Centre National des Indépendants* (1948). The CNI later became the CNIP (*Centre National des Indépendants et Paysans*) when a small peasant party merged with it.

The most dramatic development of the period was the meteoric rise of the Gaullism of the RPF (*Reassemblement du Peuple Français*) from 1947. While the regime of the Fourth Republic came under fire from the communist Left, De Gaulle launched his own campaign, which came close to the appearance of an attack from the right. He denounced the constitution and political system of the Fourth Republic as 'le régime des partis', and in place of these called for a structure in which the executive would be directly responsible to the people, in keeping with the Gaullist ideology. The RPF, he claimed, would also unite France in defence against the communists. The RPF soon claimed 1 million members, and the Fourth Republic seemed threatened from both flanks. However, the storm was weathered, an electoral system was devised for the 1951 elections to weaken the hold of communists and Gaullists, and by 1953 De Gaulle had once again retired from the political scene.

The party system after 1947 was thus affected by two new factors: firstly the rightward drift of the socialists and the Centre groups, radicals and MRP; and secondly the emergence of a Gaullist movement, claiming to stand above party and represent the whole nation.

The party system in general

With the removal of the RPF from the political scene, the pattern, on the whole, reverted to something like what it was before 1939. The mid-1950s, therefore, provide as good a vantage-point as any from which to survey a number of general features of the system, which remained largely unchanged before 1958.

The first of these is the multiplicity of the parties. This multiplicity, as we have seen, stems from the political and religious divisions created by the French Revolution, which are cut across by the division between bourgeoisie and working class, created by the growth of modern large-scale industry.

It can now also be clearly seen that, despite the multiplicity of the parties and the bewildering variety of party labels, the parties do in fact fall into ideological groups within which the continuity of attitudes over the years is striking.

Apart from their multiplicity, the other feature most noteworthy to the British eye about the French parties is that they have included such powerful anti-parliamentary groups, including a substantial proportion of the Left (the communists and the post-1968 revolutionaries), and the whole of the extreme Right. In Britain in the twentieth century, all the major parties at least have accepted the framework of parliamentary democracy, and anti-democratic parties have remained on the political fringe. In France the picture has been very different. The threat to democracy from the Fascist Leagues was taken very seriously by the Left in the 1930s, and it was widely believed that the right-wing demonstration of 6 February 1934 might lead to the fall of the Third Republic. And after the Second World War, not only the Poujadists, but De Gaulle himself, led attacks on the parliamentary system.

Equally, from its beginnings in the late nineteenth century until the 1960s, the revolutionary wing of the socialist movement as represented first by the Guesdists of the *Parti Ouvrier Français*, then from 1920 by the *Parti Communiste Français*, has for the most part remained opposed to the parliamentary system. Both parties saw parliamentary democracy as a mere tool of the bourgeoisie, and their aim at least on paper remained until 1968 to wrest political power from the bourgeoisie by insurrection and set up a purely working-class government. While the possibility of revolution seemed remote in France from the end of the last century until 1968, the Communist Party never ceased to regard itself as revolutionary, with the result that most of the time it has remained in a political ghetto, isolated from the main body of French political life and unwilling to take part in, or even support, the majority of French governments. Only during the periods of its tactical alliance with democracy against the Right — as during the Dreyfus Affair and during the years of fascist threat (1934 to 1947) — has revolutionary socialism in France been prepared to fit in with the republican system. And only since 1968 has it shown more and more itself ready to come to terms permanently with parliamentary methods, and renounce revolution. Meanwhile new revolutionaries have emerged, and the inability of both reactionary and revolutionary groups to co-exist amicably within a single political system has continued to produce an atmosphere of strife in politics that has not been paralleled in Britain.

The third important general feature of the party system in pre-1958 France was the relative weakness of the parties. Apart from the communists, few were strongly organized like their British counterparts, with annual conferences and a network of branches. On the whole they were weak, with low memberships. Maurice Duverger has drawn attention to this point, in vivid terms:

La première originalité de nos partis politiques, c'est leur faiblesse, leur infirmité. On appelle 'partis' chez nous des états-majors sans troupes, des comités sans militants, de petits groupes de notables locaux, des poignées de politiciens professionnels ou semi-professionnels, sans rapport avec les grandes organisations populaires qui portent ce nom dans les nations voisines. Seul notre parti communiste avec 400,000 adhérents fait figure internationale. Nos autres partis sont extraordinairement faibles par rapport à leurs homologues étrangers. La SFIO n'atteint pas 90,000 membres alors que la social-démocratie allemande en réunit 620,000 ... A droite et au centre, les différences sont encore plus saisissantes. Nos indépendants se réduisent à quelques milliers de notables, alors que le parti conservateur britannique compte plus de deux millions d'adhérents individuels. Le MRP ne réunit pas dix mille adhérents alors que la démocratie chrétienne allemande en groupe 280,000 et la démocratie chrétienne italienne un million et demi. (*La Démocratie sans le peuple*, Paris, Seuil, 1967, p. 7).

Many 'parties', it should be added were impermanent, being no more than electoral alliances, which collapsed immediately after the election campaign that brought them into being. This brings us to the question of the nature of party alliances — yet another general feature of the system. It is a basic fact of political life in France that no party can afford to neglect electoral alliances if it is to win the maximum number of seats in an election. With an electoral system based on a second ballot, at which the weaker candidates, who have polled the lowest number of votes on the first ballot, withdraw from the contest, the parties are forced to come to agreements with their closest political neighbours to stand down in each other's favour if their candidate comes off badly at the first ballot. Nor can a party hope to govern entirely on its own, because only once (1968) has a party ever obtained an overall majority. Finally, no candidate of any party can become President of the Republic without at least the tacit support of other parties than his own. Alliances between parties therefore inevitably spring up at election times between parties whose ideas are closest together, and who are ready to sacrifice some measure of ideological purity in order to join forces. The whole process of the formation and dissolving of party alliances in France can be seen as a result of the pressure of electoral systems on the parties; if that pressure becomes strong, and ideas are compatible, there will be an alliance; if the pressure eases off, or ideas are too far apart, the alliance will not be possible. The *Fédération de la Gauche* is a case in point: founded in 1965, it brought together a large part of the non-communist Left, under the impact of the system for the election of the President of the Republic introduced in 1962 (see below). Because communists and socialists could not yet work together, it remained a rival to the Communist Party. And when the invasion of Czechoslovakia in 1968 revived Cold War attitudes of hostility to the Soviet Union and communism, the radicals deserted the *Fédération*, simply on the grounds that the socialists were *too close to communism*. Ideological incompatibility is not an unchanging factor.

De Gaulle against the parties under the Fifth Republic

Theoretically, the coming of the Fifth Republic should have done much to alter the pattern of twentieth-century party politics in France which has just been described. For, in their traditional form, the political parties were part and parcel of the parliamentary system of government that De Gaulle had condemned as 'le régime des partis' and replaced by the system of the Fifth Republic. The essence of the parliamentary system lies in the responsibility of governments to Parliament, their continual need to obtain and keep the support of a majority of deputies in order to attain and stay in office. De Gaulle's Fifth Republic was based on quite different principles: he maintained that since governments in France before 1958 depended on constantly shifting majorities, and so were weak and unstable, they must, under the Fifth Republic, be responsible in the first place to the President. This would bring about governmental stability. It was the President who was to appoint the Prime Minister; the latter was then to submit his list of ministers to the President's approval. The support of a parliamentary majority, under the Fifth Republic, came to seem, for governments, more and more of a formality.

Parties under the parliamentary system. How should this have affected the role of the parties? The fact is that it ought to have undermined their whole purpose, for in a parliamentary democracy such as France was before 1958 it is the parties who are the basic claimants to political power, rival organizations vying with each other at elections and in Parliament to get into a favourable position to form a government either alone, or in a combination with others.

At election times, their aim is to obtain support from the electors for their candidates and a more or less specific programme, and any party winning the support of an overall majority in Parliament would expect to use its control of Parliament to set up a government to translate its ideas into action. Such a situation, though normal in Britain with its two large parties, is very rare in France. There the smaller parties can at best hope to combine their parliamentary strength to form a composite majority, obtain only a share in governmental power and see only some of their aims incorporated into the government's action. The parties, in a parliamentary democracy, thus can act as a means whereby the conflicting programmes, with which the electorate are asked to show their agreement at election time, can be channelled into coherent action. Political parties under a parliamentary system, in so far as their election programmes reflect the wishes of varying sections of the electorate, can provide a means by which the conflicting ideas and interests of various groups among the electorate can be channelled into government action.

The Gaullist alternative. De Gaulle always denied the effectiveness of the French parties in carrying out this task. He held that the parties simply could not channel the interests of the French people as a whole into coherent action: the French were too volatile, too easily led into superficial bickering on trivial issues that ignored the people's real wishes. The parties represented nothing but themselves, and so parliamentary democracy was incapable of solving France's problems. Under the Fifth Republic, he believed, both parliamentary democracy and the traditional parties had become obsolete; he dubbed the latter 'les partis de jadis'. These parties, he declared in 1962, 'lors même qu'une commune passion professionnelle les réunisse pour un instant, ne représentent pas la nation'. The governments of the past, 'ne représentant jamais autre chose que des fractions ... ne se confondaient pas avec l'intérêt général', he had asserted in 1958.

It was not the parties, or the squabbling professional politicians that led them, who could represent France; it was De Gaulle himself. The Fifth Republic was based on the notion that the ideas and interests of a France which was at bottom really united could only be channelled into action through a direct link, over the heads of the party politicians, between the French people as a whole and the person of their President. He was to become the living embodiment of national unity, as he had been in 1940. Rule through governments beholden to the parties in Parliament was to be replaced by the rule of a President, who, being responsible to the people as a whole, could appoint governments, and in times of need could consult the people, by dissolving Parliament or holding a referendum. In such a system, the parties ought to have become superfluous.

Parties and clubs under the Fifth Republic. What, in fact, happened after De Gaulle came to power in 1958? In the first place, a new Gaullist movement was set up, the UNR, to fight the 1958 and subsequent parliamentary elections. The UNR, in keeping with De Gaulle's principles, claimed to be something quite different from a party. It was officially described in about 1963 as a 'union', 'un rassemblement de familles spirituelles diverses, animé par une conception commune du destin de notre pays'. Its aim was to organize support for De Gaulle and the new constitutional system on a nationwide basis.

As for the traditional parties, De Gaulle seemed at first to have succeeded in his campaign to discredit them. While the new Gaullist movement moved electorally from weakness to strength, support drained away from communists, socialists, radicals and MRP. The total number of votes gained by all the traditional parties taken together fell from 15.6 million in 1958 to 11.8 million in 1962. The decline of the old parties was widely commented on, and there was talk of 'depolitization' in France, a decline of interest in politics itself.

But political discussion continued, at any rate on the Left: its focus shifted from the parties to the political clubs that multiplied after 1958. If the parties were discredited, discussion could continue in the clubs; if the parties were outdated the clubs could bring them up to date; if they were too dogmatic, the clubs could discuss more freely. From the outset, however, the clubs were in a dilemma over their relations with the parties. Should they seek to work alongside the parties or try to replace them? Some clubs, such as the Club Jean Moulin, made up of high civil servants and intellectuals, were hostile to the old parties and sought their renewal by the formation of new ones. Others refused to make overt political stands.

In seeking to modernize the ideas of the parties, the clubs began to adapt themselves to the new political system of the Fifth Republic, and while many of the old party leaders on the Left clung to the parliamentary ideals of the Fourth Republic, the clubs espoused in particular the new system introduced in 1962 for the election of the President by universal suffrage. This system would allow the French, they felt, to get away from the ideas and personalities of the past. They helped to launch François Mitterrand as presidential candidate for the Left in 1965.

But how far had the pattern really changed by the end of the 1960s? We have noted one important development resulting from the new constitution: in view of the continued presence of pro-Gaullist majorities in Parliament since 1958, the old pattern of shifting majorities in Parliament had been replaced by that of a regular majority, together with its corollary, a regular opposition. Parties could now be classified according to whether they belonged to the majority or the opposition.

However, the Gaullists, despite their protestations, had developed into a normal party, in so far as they fought elections and exercised political power under De Gaulle's aegis. Indeed they were, from the early 1960s until 1974, the main party of government.

Enthusiasm for Gaullism had begun to ebb, though, by 1965, and the Gaullists' claim to represent the whole nation was wearing thin: economic difficulties marred the picture of continuous economic expansion and prosperity which they projected, so that the parties of the Left experienced a revival. The new institutions in fact helped in this revival when the election of the President by universal suffrage took effect in the presidential election of 1965. The left-wing parties were allowed television time during the election campaign, and the French launched into political discussion on a scale unknown since 1958. The total poll (85 per cent) was unprecedentedly high, and it showed clearly that the 'depolitization' which had been spoken of since 1958 was a myth. The parties of the Left re-discovered something of their old role, if not yet as aspirants to government, at least as useful vehicles of protest. As early as 1963, in a public opinion poll, 64 per cent of those questioned had in fact said that the role of the parties was still 'très ou assez important', while 70 per cent still considered them 'assez ou très importants pour représenter la volonté des citoyens'. So by 1965, De Gaulle's success in taking over in person the role of the parties in representing the citizens and selecting governments, was waning. In the presidential election he was forced to a second ballot by Mitterrand, and only got back in on the second ballot by 55 per cent against 45 per cent for his left-wing opponent.

The new system for electing Presidents was, however,

affecting the relations between Left, Right and Centre. The need to form political groupings round the two candidates who could hope to oppose each other on a second ballot was having the effect of grouping the political forces of the non-communist Left around the SFIO, and the Right and part of the Centre around De Gaulle. The Centre candidate, Lecanuet, was eliminated on the first ballot in the presidential election, and the Centre votes split on the second ballot between De Gaulle and Mitterrand. A new phenomenon was thus emerging to rival the old domination of the Centre in French politics, a polarization between Left and Right, together with a splitting and squeezing out of the Centre.

This polarization process continued to dominate the political scene in the period before the 1967 elections. The socialists, radicals and clubs began to organize their joint forces for the elections in the *Fédération de la Gauche*, originally formed to support Mitterrand in 1965. The *Républicains Indépendants* of Valéry Giscard d'Estaing found themselves bound by the logic of polarization to maintain their conditional support for the orthodox Gaullists, which was expressed in the famous formula 'Oui-mais'.

The party political pattern was beginning to fall into the present-day form described at the beginning of this chapter, in which the polarization between Left and Right keeps the *Républicains Indépendants* within the Gaullist majority, whatever their desire for an independent existence, and has brought about, step-by-step, the extension of the majority towards the Centre, so that it includes to-day not only the Right but the whole of the Centre as well, leaving only the parties of the Left in opposition. This pattern of polarization between a mainly right-wing majority and a mainly left-wing opposition was at its most intense in Parliament immediately after the 1967 legislative elections, when, because of the narrowness of the Gaullist majority, both majority and opposition for a time experienced the pressures towards party discipline in what some thought was really at last beginning to move towards a *de facto* two-party system.

At last it seemed that those who had talked so earnestly since 1958 of a simplification, a regrouping of the French parties into fewer units, could hope for real change. Alas, this was a vain hope. For, as we have seen, even when parties do come

together in France, it is as a result mainly of electoral
pressures: when these pressures die down between elections,
the alliances break up, and the parties naturally fall back into
their basic ideological groupings, which have the power to
persist from decade to decade. When the French have been
and continue to be so divided on such fundamental issues as
the nature of their political regime and their economic system,
party divisions are likely to remain deep, and cooperation
between different political movements a tender plant. While
parties will come together, if ideologically compatible enough,
for short-term electoral advantage, ideological cleavages may
revive, elections may fade into the distance, and in any case
the attachment of political leaders to the individual identity of
their own formation is a powerful obstacle to any permament
fusion. All these factors were at work when the *Fédération de
la Gauche* after 1968 not only failed to turn itself into a party,
but melted away, leaving the radical party ready for a
take-over bid by Jean-Jacques Servan-Schreiber, and the
socialists in splendid isolation as they founded a 'new' party
and started a debate with the communists, which after many
hesitations culminated in the drawing up of a joint
government programme for the elections of 1973. The
electoral 'need' for the socialists to combine with the radicals
disappeared, while affinities grew with the communists, as the
latter gradually shed the last of their reservations over
parliamentary methods. The division between the communists
and the non-communist Left, which had been a deep one ever
since the split at Tours in 1920, was on the way to being
healed, as a result of internal changes in the Communist Party.
Progress in the 'de-Stalinization' of the party had been slow,
certainly; Thorez, the old guard leader, remained in office
until his death in 1964, and the new party statutes introduced
in that year hardly marked a great step towards internal
democracy in the party. On the other hand, doctrinal moves
towards the acceptance of a 'passage pacifique au socialisme'
seemed to point to a retreat from revolutionary violence, as did
the new readiness to accept that democratic socialism might be
allowed to coexist with communism through the whole period
of change-over to socialism. The fears of the socialists of the
SFIO that to collaborate with the communists could only be a
prelude to being completely absorbed by them were somewhat

allayed, and an electoral pact was signed between communists and socialists at the end of 1966, after the first top-level talks since 1947. At the time of the 1967 elections, the new softening of the communist line was accompanied by declarations of readiness to accept governmental responsibilities. Declarations such as these were taken quite seriously by the French public, which was preparing, for its part, to welcome the communists back into the fabric of French political life. The culmination of the process of re-integration for the communists came during and after May 1968, when they fought shy of revolution. By 1970-2, the socialists had shed all their hesitations and a new alliance was born, one with infinitely greater electoral attractions than that represented by the *Fédération*, and one that was, by now, within the limits of political compatibility.

On the eve of the events of May 1968, the political parties seemed, in short, to have changed very little, despite the coming of the Fifth Republic and a new Gaullist movement; many of the factors governing their relations were the traditional ones which have been described. As for the 'modernization' which had been talked of: the Gaullists' ideas were not all that much different from those with which the General had launched the RPF in 1947; the communists were changing, it is true, but for the non-communist Left 'modernization' seemed to mean no more than a growing acceptance, with reservations, of the political system of the Fifth Republic, and a coming to terms with the mixed economy, part publicly owned, part capitalist, in the hope that social inequalities could be ironed out within the existing system through the rises in the standard of living created by ever greater expansion resulting from economic planning. As the programme of the *Fédération de la Gauche* put it, the need was for 'une politique économique et sociale visant à élever le plus rapidement possible le niveau de vie du plus grand nombre, à établir une répartition plus équitable du revenu national, à répondre en priorité aux besoins essentiels de la culture et des loisirs, de la santé et de l'habitat ... Pour atteindre ces grands objectifs, une croissance économique élevée, le maintien du pouvoir d'achat de la monnaie et une stricte orientation de la production sont nécessaires. Le Plan constitue l'instrument d'une telle politique' (*L'Année politique 1965*, pp. 442-3). This 'modern' policy seemed closer to conservation than innovation; it was an attempt to arrest the growth of public ownership at the point it had reached in 1945.

A new dimension of economic and social conflict

As 1968 approached, however, fundamental social changes were beginning to foreshadow the arrival of a new factor to complicate the party political pattern anew: the re-emergence of anti-parliamentary groups, in the shape of a new extreme Left, threatening to outflank the Communist Party on its left, as it became integrated into the system, much as the socialists themselves had outflanked the republicans at the end of last century, when they settled down as conservatives to defend the system.

What were these social changes? As some percipient sociologists were beginning to point out, managerial authority, in the large-scale industrial units that multiplied in post-war France, had become a more immediately oppressive feature than mere ownership. The old conflict between the worker and the capitalist, which had been at the root of the economic division between left-wing and right-wing parties for many decades, was being overshadowed by a new, or new-seeming, conflict between the worker and the manager. This change in the nature of economic conflict was paralleled by the proliferation of large bureaucratic structures outside the sphere of production: in the professions, and education, in business, in administration, and, of course, in politics itself. The individual at the base more often than not found himself or herself in conflict with remote and impersonal authority.

The revolt of 1968 constituted an attack, which spread from the students to young professional people, and some at least of the younger workers, against authoritarian social, economic and political structures in all their forms. As Servan-Schreiber put it:

> Ce qu'il met en cause, ce n'est pas la propriété, qui est traitée comme un problème accessoire, mais au premier chef, le *pouvoir* et l'authorité ... Ce mouvement est d'abord une mise en question radicale des formes présentes de l'autorité — à limite de toute autorité. On y distingue

une manifestation classique du démon français de l'anarchie.
(*Le Réveil de la France*, Paris, Denoël, 1968, p. 44.)

Politically, this attack can best be characterized as a vigorous
shift away from the century-old doctrines of communism and
socialism in the direction of the ideas of anarchism. Socialism
and communism on the traditional pattern, while they were
concerned to change the ownership of the means of
production, were quite prepared to accommodate to structures
of centralized state authority, indeed to capture and use them,
at least temporarily, in order to introduce socialism. Whereas
the political movements thrown up by May 1968, whatever
their confusing variety of labels, their broad division into
Maoists, Trotskyists and anarchists, had at least one thing in
common — their refusal to subordinate to centralized state
authority the ideas and interests of the people, the refusal that
these should be channelled through the dictatorial personality
of a De Gaulle, or even through Communist Party dictatorship, or a socialist party working within a structure of
parliamentary democracy. Here was a rejection of the role
of the traditional political party far more radical than De
Gaulle's attempt to confiscate for one man the task of
channelling popular wishes. Socialism and communism on the
old model stood condemned, as they had been for a century or
more by the successors of Proudhon's anarchism, since they
must inevitably descend into demagogy, and are always
dogged, to a greater or lesser extent, by internal bureaucracy.
It was therefore natural that the Socialist and Communist
Parties should have been and remain hostile to the
revolutionary movement which emerged in May 1968, and
should be accused by the revolutionaries of an attempt to take
advantage of the May events to ride back into power on their
backs.

The revolutionaries of 1968 were agreed about one point:
the need to avoid the bureaucracy that political parties bring
with them, a bureaucracy that was seen at its worst in Stalinist
communism in eastern Europe, but which also dogged
communism and socialism in the West. They aimed, in the
political sphere, at various forms of direct democracy which
largely do away with the need for political parties: rotation of
citizens in office, to avoid elected persons becoming professional demagogues; or immediate recall by the electors of their

representatives if they do not act in accordance with their
electors' wishes. Both these systems express a characteristic
left-wing demand for greater popular control of government
which is in keeping with the most extreme developments of the
1789 Revolution: they illustrate the scope for political ideas to
the left of those of socialists and communists tied to the notion
of party. In the industrial sphere, the new extreme Left born
of 1968 finds a good deal of common ground in the idea of a
socialist society based on *autogestion* or self-management by
the workers through workers' councils, in which the elected
representatives of the workers will manage the processes of
production for themselves. Common ownership of the means
of production, as in old-style socialism and communism, is not
enough in itself: it may simply lead to a centralized economic
bureaucracy. It must, on the new view, be accompanied by
decentralized popular control of production.

These ideas have spread from the revolutionary groups.
They evoked a strong response from the PSU in 1968, for that
party had been founded in 1968 by disillusioned ex-communists
and others already seeking an alternative to bureaucratic
socialism. The PSU has now made *autogestion* the main plank
of its programme. Direct democracy and *autogestion* have
become the touch-stones of the groups of the revolutionary
extreme Left. Their concessions to parliamentary methods are
limited, through, as we have seen, the PSU got a foot in
Parliament in 1969, and the Trotskyist *Ligue Communiste* put
up candidates in 1973. Their home is at present outside
Parliament and outside the system, though the question
remains whether they will not at some time in the future
become integrated into a changed society, as their predecessors
have in the past, ever since 1789. In so far as they are more
alien to a state structure of any kind so far set up in the West
than even the communists, they may, on the other hand, be
heading for a long period of agitation outside the system;
certainly the mutual hostility between them and the Communist Party remains as lively as in 1968. Yet the socialists and
even, to a minute extent, the communists have not remained
unaffected by their ideas, since by 1972 the Socialist Party's
programme was talking of *autogestion* as a long-term aim, and
the word actually appears in the communist-socialist joint
programme as well, though the communists are careful to

dissociate themselves from it. However, these moves towards self-management, like the talk of 'participation' on the Gaullist Right and in the Centre — a continuation of the compromises with capitalism characteristic of the Centre — are superficial, since the ideas of the extreme Left are as incompatible with socialism and communism based on a centralized state and economy as they are with the dictatorial tendencies of Gaullism. And Gaullism, too, refuses to take any major steps towards decentralizing the state. The closest the older parties came to the new way of thinking, at least in the political sphere, was when the Radical Party came under Servan-Schreiber's leadership from 1970. In 1968, Servan-Schreiber identified himself with the revolt against authority, and by 1970 had launched, in his manifesto *Ciel et Terre*, a far-reaching attack on political authority structures, carrying the Radical Party with him. He then extended his ideas to embrace extreme regional decentralization, another issue characteristic of the new extreme left, and was accused by the Gaullists of trying to 'dismantle the state'. His extremism did not extend to economics, however, and he fought shy of any all-out attack on capitalism. This is why he landed up in the political centre in 1971, in alliance with Jean Lecanuet in the *Mouvement Réformateur*, and found his way into M. Giscard d'Estaing's government, and why the left-wing radicals, who have always had a tendency towards socialism, abandoned him to join the communist-socialist alliance. The radicals' political extremism and economic moderation under Servan-Schreiber gives them an intermediate outlook, characteristic of the Centre.

By 1977, the parties of the Left at least seemed to have moved measurably away from their 1958 positions: in twelve years, the impetus of de-Stalinization had taken the communists wholly into the orbit of parliamentary methods, and despite much bickering, caused by their fears that the rapidly growing socialists would overtake them electorally, they seemed fairly permanently committed to the alliance with the socialists and the *radicaux de gauche* within the *Union de la Gauche*. The Left, above all, now seemed to be within hailing distance of political power, for the first time since before 1958. All the formations of the non-communist Left had gone a long way towards absorbing the notion of *autogestion*, inherited from

1968, and were, too, on the road to an awareness of the equally significant issues of decentralization and ecology.

The Gaullists of the UDR had lost their last foot-hold on the commanding heights of political power when M. Chirac was replaced as prime minister by M. Raymond Barre, and their capacity to find a new rôle when shorn both of De Gaulle and political power looked as if it would be severely tested in the run-up to the 1978 legislative elections. M. Chirac gained a point, however, when he was elected mayor of Paris in the March 1977 municipal elections, and the appeal of his antisocialism remained arguably stronger than M. Giscard d'Estaing's promises of reform, as fears grew within a divided majority that the Left's sweeping gains in the municipal elections were a prelude to an election victory in 1978, and perhaps the demise of the Fifth Republic.

Bibliography

General. A general historical introduction is provided by Siegfried, A., *Tableau des partis en France*, Paris, Grasset, 1930; translated as *France: a Study in Nationality*, New Haven, Yale University Press, 1930; while Goguel, F., *La politique des partis sous la Troisième République*, Paris, Seuil, 1946, is the outstanding treatment of French party politics before 1939.

Williams, P.M., *Crisis and Compromise*. London, Longmans, 1964. Provides essays on the parties before 1958 which are authoritative, as it is the whole treatment of the Fourth Republic.

Chapsal, J., *La vie politique en France depuis 1940*, including exhaustive bibliographies on the parties, and many references to the studies on the parties published regularly by the *Revue française de science politique*, which should always be consulted on the latest developments.

Ehrmann, H.W., *Politics in France*. Boston, Little Brown, 1971 (second edition). The most stimulating and knowledgeable single volume account of French politics. It has an emphasis on political sociology. Very rewarding for any student of France, and well worth the trouble of getting to grips with, even for the newcomer to French politics.

Ambler, J.S., *The Government and Politics of France*. Boston, Houghton Mifflin, 1971. Includes much the clearest and most up-to-date introduction to the fundamentals of French party politics for the student.

Pickles, D.M., *The Government and Politics of France*, London, Methuen, 1972, supersedes the author's *Fifth French Republic*, and provides an up-to-date picture of the parties and the governmental system in France with a wealth of detail.

L'Année politique reproduces party manifestoes and political speeches and deals, in its annual volumes, with most major developments affecting the parties. Its chronological arrangement and full index make it an ideal lead-in to detailed research in *Le Monde* or other French newspapers. An up-to-date collection of newspaper cuttings on the French parties and other political topics can be found in the library of the Institut d'Etudes Politiques at 27 rue St Guillaume, Paris 7e.

The Annual Register of World Events includes, each year, an invaluable essay on political events in France, most useful for very recent developments affecting the parties. *Keesing's Archives* also provides useful, reliable and up-to-date detail in English.

Parties. Among the shorter groups of essays on the parties the most satisfactory are in Duverger, M., *Institutions politiques et droit constitutionnel*, Paris, PUF, 1970 (eleventh edition completely rewritten), which includes very full bibliographies on the parties; and in Goguel, F. and Grosser, A., *La Politique en France*, Paris, Colin, 1975 (fifth edition), which gives recent election statistics. Borella, P., *Les partis politiques dans la France d'aujourd'hui*, Paris, Seuil, 1975 (second edition, up-to-date as at 1 November 1974) is essential for its solid, analysis of the parties and the party system.

Duverger, M., *La Démocratie sans le peuple*. Paris, Seuil, 1967. Most stimulating for its provocative, yet, to me, convincing emphasis on the Centre. His earlier book, *Partis politiques et classes sociales*, Paris, Colin, 1955, is basic on the social composition of the parties.

Cahm, E., *Politics and Society in Contemporary France 1789-1971: A Documentary History*. London, Harrap, 1972.

Traces by means of documents in French the evolution of the parties — and other social and political phenomena — since the nineteenth century. There are introductory essays in English and bibliographies on each party. (Available in paperback as *Politique et société*. Paris, Flammarion, 1977.)

Duverger, M., *Constitutions et documents politiques*, Paris, PUF, 1968, reproduces the statutes of the political parties and gives full electoral statistics for the twentieth century.

On individual parties and groups see:

Pfister, T., *Tout savoir sur le gauchisme*. Paris, Filipacchi, 1972.

Guerin, D., *L'anarchisme*. Paris, Gallimard, 1965.

Gombin, R., *Les origines du gauchisme*. Paris, Seuil, 1971. Translated as *The Origins of Modern Leftism*. London, Penguin Books, 1975.

Kriegel, A., *Les Communistes*. Paris, Seuil, 1968. Translated as *The French Communists: Profile of a People*. University of Chicago Press, 1972.

Programme commun de gouvernement du parti communiste français et du parti socialiste (*27 juin 1972*). Paris, Editions Sociales, 1972.

Philip, A., *Les socialistes*. Paris, Seuil, 1967.

Nania, G., *Le PSU avant Rocard*. Paris, Roblot, 1973.

Guidoni, P., *Histoire du nouveau parti socialiste*. Paris, Téma, 1973.

Nicolet, C., *Le radicalisme*. Paris, PUF, 1967.

Servan-Schreiber, J.-J. and Albert, M., *Ciel et terre: manifeste radical*. Paris, Denoël, 1970.

Irving, R.E.M., *Christian Democracy in France*. London, Allen & Unwin, 1973.

Rémond, R., *La Droite en France de la Première Restauration à la Ve République*, 2 vols. Paris, Aubier-Montaigne, 1968 (third edition). Translated as *The Right Wing in France*. London and Philadelphia, Oxford University Press and Pennsylvania State University Press, 1968. Fundamental on all aspects of the Right; includes an appendix on May 1968 and many documents.

Colliard, J.-C., *Les Républicains Indépendants*. Paris, PUF, 1972. A full scholarly study.

Charlot, J., *Le phénomène gaulliste*. Paris, Seuil, 1970. Translated as *The Gaullist Phenomenon*. London, Allen & Unwin, 1970. Basic on Gaullism as are the documents in the same author's *Le Gaullisme*. Paris, Colin, 1970.

Avril, P., *UDR et gaullistes*. Paris, PUF, 1971. Useful documents.

Chiroux, R., *L'extrême droite sous la Ve République*. Paris, LGDJ, 1974.

3 Trade unions

Malcolm Anderson

Introduction

'Working-class unity' is a slogan which has always been popular on the Left in France. But unity has been a mirage for the trade union movement, constantly beckoning but always beyond its reach. The divisions within the movement go back to its nineteenth-century origins, and although at certain times the climate has apparently been favourable to a greater degree of unity little has been achieved until recent years. The most important organization at the national level, the *Confédération Générale du Travail* (CGT) founded in 1895, has never succeeded in bringing together all the important unions and has itself split three times, in 1921, 1939 and 1948. In the twentieth century pressures towards greater unity have always been counter-balanced by divisive factors. The coming together of the various strands of French socialism to form the *Section Français de l'Internationale Ouvrière* in 1905 was an encouragement to greater unity in the trade union movement. But the opportunity was lost because, at that time, the CGT was dominated by revolutionary syndicalists who despised the socialists who participated in parliamentary politics and alarmed the more moderate members of the working class. The great enthusiasm of 1936, when a left-wing coalition, the Popular Front, won an electoral victory produced results. The CGT was reunited, but within three years the communist and socialist wings parted company because the signing of the Nazi-Soviet pact in 1939 divided them so deeply. The great and widely shared suffering of trade unionists during the Second World War re-established a sense of solidarity, but this quickly broke down in the post-war period when the cold war caused considerable rancour between communist and non-communist in French working-class politics.

The contemporary divisions in the trade union movement date from the late 1940s. The largest organization at the national level was, and remains, the CGT, although in terms of membership it has never reacquired the position it had in the Liberation period. The two main rivals to the CGT were the *Confédération Générale du Travail-Force Ouvrière* and the *Confédération Française des Travailleurs Chrétiens*. The CGT-FO was established in 1948 by socialists, reformists and syndicalists who did not wish to participate in a communist-led trade union confederation. The CFTC was much older: it was founded in 1919 as the culmination of previous initiatives by social Catholic pioneers such as Count Albert de Mun and René de La Tour du Pin who founded the *Cercles Ouvriers* in the 1870s, and Christian trade unionists such as Jules Zirnheld who, prior to 1914, had been very active in white collar unions. The CFTC originally catered for Christian trade unionists, whether Catholic or Protestant, and was greatly influenced by papal teaching on the social question. But it gradually lost its confessional character and severed its last links with the church when, in 1964, it changed its name to the *Confédération Française Démocratique du Travail*. A few of the old guard Christian trade unionists objected to the change and formed a breakaway confederation with the old name, the CFTC, but the membership of this was little more than one-tenth of that of the CFDT. In addition to the big three confederations, there have been a number of other important organizations which have had a continuous history since the late 1940s. The next largest is a trade union federation which is not affiliated to a confederation: this is the *Fédération de l'Education Nationale* which has grown in size with the rapid expansion of the teaching profession since the Second World War. The *Confédération Générale des Cadres*, composed mainly of managerial, scientific and technical staffs, was founded in 1944 by unions which did not like the political affiliations of the other confederations or considered them insufficiently committed to maintaining wage and salary differentials. Other more minor organizations include the *Confédération des Syndicats Indépendants*, *Confédération des Syndicats Autonomes* and a number of unions which are so independent and so autonomous that they will not even affiliate to these organizations.

The trade union movement presents a picture of division and fragmentation, but this is not at all uncommon in western Europe. The united movements of Germany, Austria and the United Kingdom are not the norm and situations similar to the French exist in Holland, Belgium, Switzerland and Italy. The trade union movements of Spain and Portugal show signs of similar fragmentation as freedom of association is being restored in those countries. In all the countries with a fragmented trade union movement there are deep political cleavages based on social, geographical and ideological factors: the splintering of the political Left into several parties almost always accompanies divisions within the trade union movement even though there may be no organizational ties between unions and parties. In the French case the revolutionary tradition, the religious factor and the location of industry are the main elements in the environment of the trade unions which have supported divisions between them. In the late eighteenth and the nineteenth centuries political changes were successfully carried through by revolution and this created an aspiration in broad sectors of the working class to achieve fundamental social change by revolutionary means. This aspiration was sealed in blood when 'bourgeois' governments during the Second Republic and in the Paris commune of 1871 put down left-wing proletarian movements by force. The nineteenth-century experiences are at the origin of the fundamental split in the working class between revolutionaries and reformists. The survival of religious practice in some working-class communities, particularly in the north and east, until the twentieth century also divided worker from worker because in the estimation of the revolutionary Left, religion was fundamentally reactionary. Although the climate has radically altered since the beginning of the twentieth century when the clerical question dominated domestic political debate, the very different kinds of general outlook of men who, however tenuously, are associated with the revolutionary and Christian traditions has helped to maintain a major division within the trade union movement.

The economic development of France has also been a

divisive factor. In the nineteenth and in the first half of the twentieth century the French working class was more isolated and dispersed than the British or the German. It was divided between the heavy concentrations of industry around Paris and along the northern and eastern frontiers, and scattered pockets elsewhere in a country dominated by the small town and the countryside. Both situations tended to produce a ghetto complex in the working class, a feeling of being in a minority situation and relatively powerless in the existing political and social order. There were many expressions of this feeling in the highly emotional outbursts of working-class frustration which have punctuated the social history of France. In the various industrial areas very different industrial conditions prevailed and the persistence of a large number of small- and medium-sized firms created very different local situations.

Economic changes in the last two decades have altered these basic features of the French industrial system and modified the context in which the trade unions are operating. The size of the agricultural sector has declined and industry has become more dispersed. France has become a genuinely industrial society; the political and social influence of the peasants and country-dwellers has radically diminished in the last quarter of a century. Large industrial firms such as Rhône-Poulenc, Renault-Peugeot, Saint-Gobain-Péchiney and Michelin are dominating the economy to an ever greater extent. A long period of fairly steady industrial growth has given all sections of the community new confidence and optimism about their future prospects. Expansion and prosperity has resulted in increased social and geographical mobility; class and regional barriers have been eroding. The once extraordinary regional and local differences in wage rates have been narrowing. There is greater uniformity in the work situation over the whole country and the prospect of steady material improvements. All these factors affect trade union organization and outlook, but the influence of the sediment left by the past is nonetheless strong.

Ideology and trade unionism

On the surface, differing political philosophies seem to be the major cause of division within the trade union movement.

Catholics, reformists, socialists, syndicalists and communists have refused to cooperate because they have differed about the purpose of human society. The importance of the ideological factor as a cause of division is uncertain and assessment of it must finally be a matter of personal judgement. But the influence of the various ideological strands has certainly changed over time. The dominant political theory of the heroic age of the trade union movement at the turn of the twentieth century, revolutionary syndicalism, survives only among small minorities. Revolutionary syndicalism of the period 1900-10 was less a consistent political theory and more a mood and set of attitudes. Its main proposition was that the *syndicats* ought to be the basis of a new social order which would come into being after a revolutionary general strike.

The Charter of Amiens, approved by the CGT congress of 1906, is the best known and most influential statement of syndicalist doctrine. It was simultaneously revolutionary and reformist:

> Dans l'œuvre revendicatrice, quotidienne, le syndicalisme poursuit la coordination des efforts ouvriers, l'accroissement du mieux-être des travailleurs par les réalisations immédiates, telles que la diminution des heures de travail, l'augmentation des salaires, etc., ...
>
> Mais cette besogne n'est qu'un côté de l'œuvre du syndicalisme; il prépare l'émancipation intégrale, qui ne peut se réaliser que par l'expropriation capitaliste; il préconise comme moyen d'action la grève générale et il considère que le syndicat, aujourd'hui groupement de résistance, sera, dans l'avenir, le groupement de production et de répartition, base de réorganisation sociale.

This vision of a general strike followed by a society organized and controlled by the *syndicats*, coupled with a degree of violence in strikes, alarmed the middle classes of the 'belle époque', and various repressive measures were taken by governments against the CGT. Repression and lack of success caused revolutionary fervour to decline in the years immediately preceding the First World War. Under the skilful leadership of Léon Jouhaux, general secretary of the CGT from 1909 to 1947 and subsequently president of the CGT-FO, the movement was converted to a more reformist approach and concentrated on limited practical objectives. Elements of revolutionary syndicalism survived in most of the major unions; during major strikes and social upheavals, such as the events of May 1968, the atmosphere of revolutionary syndicalism is revived.

A great ideological divide appeared after the First World War caused by the foundation of the Communist Party. The success of the Bolshevik revolution in Russia in 1917 had immediate repercussions in France, causing a schism in the SFIO between those who wanted to join the Third (Leninist) International and those who wished to follow a parliamentary road to socialism. This split was confirmed at the SFIO conference of Tours in 1920, after which the *Parti Communiste Français* was established. This new political division on the Left had important consequences for the trade union movement because the Leninist view of trade unions became very influential. Lenin believed that the trade unions had a subordinate role and that they could only engage effectively in the struggle against capitalism under the direction of a revolutionary proletarian political party; their function was to raise the level of class consciousness and help the Communist Party to keep in touch with the current preoccupations of the working class. According to Lenin, trade unions, left to themselves, engaged either in the narrow pursuit of material gains or in disorderly and ineffective agitation of the anarcho-syndicalist type. 'Trade union consciousness' was, in the Leninist vocabulary a term of abuse applied to the attitudes of those who worked through the existing system to defend professional interests. Lenin advised communists not to break with, but to work through, trade unions controlled by their political adversaries in order to promote working-class unity and prepare the way for the leadership of the Communist Party. Reformists and social democrats objected very strongly both to the substance of this point of view and the aggressive way in which it was expressed. They determined not to be taken over by the communists. After violent debates and incidents the communists were turned out of the CGT and they established the *Confédération Générale du Travail Unitaire* in September 1921. Since that time relations of trust and respect have been difficult to establish between communist and non-communist trade unionists. In the 1930s, when the Soviet

Union became alarmed by the threat of fascism, the CGTU and the PCF sought alliances with other working-class groups in order to strengthen the international working-class struggle against the dictators. Indeed, until the 1960s, the international situation and, more specifically, the exigencies of Soviet foreign policy have seemed to determine the degree to which communists could cooperate with non-communists in the trade union movement. In the 1930s and during the Second World War the numerical strength of the communists in the movement grew rapidly because of their militancy, good organization and outstanding Resistance record.

After 1945, the communists had the upper hand and, when the CGT split as a result of the Cold War, it was the non-communists who, this time, were excluded. The men who established the CGT-FO in 1948 often became bitter anti-communists and made many complaints about communist behaviour. Chief amongst these was that the communist leadership of the CGT constantly called on trade unionists to adopt political positions which had little to do with their professional interests. The political strikes of the Cold War period, which followed the exclusion of communist ministers from the French government in 1947, were regarded as particularly intolerable. The second major complaint was that communist-led unions were controlled by party cells: the democratically elected officials and committees were a facade behind which the party took all the major decisions. The third was that the CGT leadership took too much notice of the claims of non-unionized labour, always the majority of the French working class, because of its general political strategy. The communists wished to unite the working class and raise the level of class consciousness; with these aims in view they could not ignore non-unionized workers. Political developments outside France also made non-communists very suspicious of the communists. The former did not wish to see the kind of regime that had been installed in eastern Europe introduced into France. The Prague *coup* of 1948, when the communists subverted a coalition government in which they were members, increased the fears about communist methods. The complaints and fears have had much less substance in recent years but the men who now hold the senior positions in both the CGT and the CGT-FO all lived through the period of acute tension and conflict in the late 1940s and early 1950s. Relatively small conflicts can revive deep suspicions, and there is virtually no hope of reunification of the CGT whilst the present generation of leaders remain in office.

The CGT and the CGT-FO have common ideological roots in Marxism and syndicalism but the CFDT originated in an entirely different ideological tradition. Christian trade unionism was born of the desire to apply Christian principles to industrial relations. In the late nineteenth century many Catholics considered that workers should participate in the same union as the employers. Experiments on these lines were not a great success, but many Catholic employers encouraged Catholic workers' unions as a more desirable alternative to unions dominated by Marxists and syndicalists. The goodwill of some paternalist employers was not, however, a great advantage and Christian trade unionism was slow to gain a foothold in working-class milieux, even those in which traditions of Christian practice survived. Although CFTC militants were involved in strikes and other kinds of agitation, provoking a celebrated but ineffective complaint by the president of the Roubaix-Tourcoing textile consortium to the Vatican about their activities, the prejudice against Catholic trade unionism persisted for a long time among left-wing workers. Officially adhering to the doctrine of cooperation between employers and workers in a spirit of Christian fraternity, the CFTC was suspected of playing the employers' game. In the inter-war period the general political outlook of the leaders of the CFTC was so different from the CGT and CGTU that there was little possibility of cooperation between them except on limited objectives. The CFTC unions were reformists who did not accept the idea of the class struggle. They wanted various kinds of state intervention to promote social justice and modest reforms of industrial organization to give workers a share in management of firms and in their profits. Their main inspiration came from a progressive social Catholic tradition, originating in the ideas of Abbé Lammenais in the first half of the nineteenth century and from the great papal pronouncements in favour of social justice contained in the encyclicals *Rerum novarum* (1891) and *Quadragesimo anno* (1931). Many conservative Catholics thought the Catholic trade union militants went far beyond a reasonable interpretation of the guidelines laid down in these encyclicals, and the trade unionists, on their side, gradually became more and more irked by the confessional connection which they considered was limiting their freedom of action. From the late 1920s some of the more forward looking Catholic trade unionists considered that the overt connection with the church unnecessarily limited the development of their strategy and the attractiveness of their unions to potential recruits. Religious considerations need not, in their view, be invoked when groups of workers cooperated to promote their interests. This attitude became gradually more and more widely shared until, in 1964, with the change of name from CFTC to CFDT, the last vestiges of the confessional connection were dropped. Severing the ties with the church left the CFDT without a commonly agreed body of doctrine. This has made the confederation relatively receptive to new ideas and new ways of doing things. Various reformist, socialist and even revolutionary tendencies have been competing for influence and the confederation has, in general, given the impression of shifting to the Left. Whilst the other two main confederations have been expressing doctrines which go back to their origins, the CFDT appears lively and innovating.

Trade union organization

There is not any very obvious connection between the doctrines and the organization of trade unions, but ordinary trade union members clearly prefer that there is a fairly high degree of political or doctrinal harmony between the leadership and themselves. This is partly because major strikes in France usually start by militant action at the grass roots, but negotiations bringing strikes to a conclusion are frequently at a very high level, on an industry-wide basis or at national level often with the participation of the government. It follows from this relative centralization of bargaining about wages and conditions that workers are reluctant to be absorbed into larger confederations with possibly unsympathetic and remote leaders, and in which their voice could only be heard with difficulty. The overt political beliefs of many trade union leaders imply strategies and attitudes towards negotiation which workers, not sharing the same beliefs, may regard as being against their interests. For example, the CGT belief that a united working class should be seen confronting the government and the employers implies that all negotiations should be removed to the national level as quickly and as often as possible. The white collar worker or the technician in the CGT-FO or CFDT may see little point of such confrontations because he does not believe in the class struggle and, moreover, may believe that they are harmful to his particular interests which are more likely to be ignored in favour of very general working-class demands. Thus doctrine and interest combine to support the divisions in the trade union movement.

The centralization of bargaining often gives a false impression that the union leaders control the union. They often appear as authoritative spokesmen, but the extent to which they can control or mobilize the membership is quite limited. This is now true of the CGT unions, although in the 1930s and 1940s their leaders had a more commanding position. The dependence of the leaders on the membership is the product of low membership of trade unions and of some decentralization in the constitutional structure. The divisions of the unions clearly discourage membership: the united CGT had, in 1947, almost five and a half million members, whereas in the 1970s it is unlikely that the total membership of all trade unions reaches that figure. Pressure to join unions is less strong when unions are divided and a closed shop policy becomes almost impossible. Accurate membership statistics are difficult to establish because of the constant movement in and out of unions. CGT unions probably have a current membership of about one and a half million, the CGT-FO and the CFDT each have about five to six hundred thousand, and they are followed by the *Fédération de l'Education Nationale* with about four hundred thousand. Membership varies from time to time depending on the prevailing climate: crises and successful strikes usually, but not always, lead to an increase in membership. If union members object to the actions of the leaders or believe that they are ineffective, they simply let their membership lapse. In some major factories where there is a militant work force as in big firms such as Renault and Berliet it is almost as difficult to drop out of a union as it is in Britain; but these factories are not numerous. The 'following' of the trade unions is much more numerous than their membership:

many non-members can be regarded as being within the sphere of influence of one of the major unions. The so-called 'social elections', which took place until 1967 to elect the management committees of the social security system, showed that the following the major confederations had among non-unionized workers was roughly proportionate to the size of their membership. Most non-unionized workers were prepared to vote for candidates put up by the major confederations, and the CGT candidates attracted comfortable majorities in both public and private industry. This is evidence that non-members feel that the unions in some sense represent their interests. From the union's point of view, having a larger following than membership is a source of weakness. The 'followers' are much less committed to solidarity with the union than the members and they give no financial support. French trade unions are poor by international standards and have never had enough money to support strikers during major strikes. Major strikes, therefore, almost always are the result of great pent-up frustrations on the shop-floor, rather than tactical moves on the part of the trade union leadership. Lack of strike funds has also made French trade unionists expert organizers of the *grève perlée* (the go-slow), *grève de zèle* (the work to rule) and the *grève tournante* (shutting down one plant after another in an unpredictable way).

Despite low membership and lack of funds, there is considerable activity at the grass roots level of French trade unions focused on the *syndicats* and the *bourses du travail*. Historically, the trade union movement grew out of the *syndicats* which are the equivalent of the union local branch in Britain. The *syndicats* are still the basic organizational unit on which the whole structure of the movement is based. They are grouped into *unions* in the *départements* and *fédérations* at the national level. These unions and federations must, according to a law of March 1920, group together similar or related trades such as the Printing and Publishing Federation and the Civil Service Federation. The law of 1920 gives trade unions broad rights provided that they conform to this rule and provided also that they engage mainly in the pursuit of professional interests. Amongst the rights the law confers are the rights to strike and protest, issue warnings and make representations to the state and to private employers. They are 'corporate persons' who can acquire property, enter contracts and take legal action to defend members' individual and collective interests. The basic rights of trade unions were written into the preamble to the Constitution of 1946 which was reaffirmed in the Constitution of the Fifth Republic:

> Chacun a le devoir de travailler et le droit d'obtenir un emploi. Nul ne peut être lésé, dans son travail ou son emploi, en raison de ses origines, de ses opinions ou de ses croyances.
>
> Tout homme peut défendre ses droits et ses intérêts par l'action syndicale et adhérer au syndicat de son choix.
>
> Le droit de grève s'exerce dans le cadre des lois qui le réglementent.
>
> Tout travailleur participe, par l'intermédiaire de ses délégués à la détermination collective des conditions de travail aussi qu'à la gestion des entreprises.

After a long period of legal discrimination — associations of workers and employers were prohibited by the famous Le Chapellier law of 1791 and trade unions only acquired a legal basis in the 1884 law of associations — the trade unions have acquired a strong position in law.

The *bourses du travail* are also well established in law and in practice although they quickly came to have purposes which were not intended by those who founded them. The *bourses* are a peculiarly French institution which came into existence at the end of the nineteenth century. The first was created by the Paris municipal council in 1886, to provide the *syndicats* with offices, meeting rooms and a library. The *bourses* were intended to bring the *syndicats* under the influence of the municipality and the mayor. This attempt to bring the *syndicats* into close contact with the state administration and to domesticate them politically was a total failure: the *bourses* became bastions of men who vigorously defended trade union independence. Alarmed conservatives charged that anarchists, socialists and syndicalists used them to plan revolution at public expense. In times of crisis the *bourses* have often been the focus of revolutionary meetings and demonstrations, but they are more frequently used for more mundane purposes. They provide educational and friendly society services for members and act as employment exchanges. Members of all trade unions use the *bourses*, and in the places where they have been lively centres of trade union activity they have often promoted a grass roots consensus amongst members of different confederations, encouraging unity of action.

Relations with government and parties

The representative functions of the main federations and confederations are very important. Those regarded as 'most representative' send delegates to a large number of official bodies. The status of being 'most representative' is conferred by the state and can be challenged before the administrative courts. Not surprisingly, there have been a large number of cases because the status confers considerable advantages. Perhaps the most important of these is not connected with membership of official bodies but with negotiating rights. A collective agreement concluded by one of the most representative unions can be subject to an extension procedure which makes it compulsory for the whole industry.

Official spokesmen of trade unions are to be found in a large number of places in government and the public sector of the economy. They are on the boards of nationalized industries and thus participate in important management decisions. In the civil service they are involved in management and advisory committees such as the Higher Civil Service Council, the Higher Collective Agreements Committee and the *comités mixtes paritaires* (joint staff and management committees which deal with personnel and other matters). They have a voice in economic planning through representatives on the national and regional economic planning councils. They also have some influence over the management and the administration of the economy through the many joint consultative committees which cluster around the French economic and social ministries, as they do around most modern national administrations. Trade union representatives sit on the Economic and Social Council which is a kind of third advisory chamber of parliament which reviews legislation and makes reports on economic and social questions. At the international level, the trade unions send delegations to the European Economic and Social Council, which aspires to service the European Community in the same way as the equivalent

Council serves the French national government, and to the International Labour Office in Geneva.

The trade unions have not always made efficient use of the opportunities available to them through their membership of these bodies. Their divisions and weakneses are well known to those who oppose their point of view and, consequently, their opinions are often not taken seriously. Also, because of their poverty, they have not been able to employ sufficiently large research staffs to prepare their case thoroughly. This has often placed them at a serious disadvantage by comparison with the employers when they are trying to influence the content of legislation and the administration of policy. Despite this, their places on official, advisory and planning bodies are invaluable to the trade unions because divisions in the movement and among the political parties of the Left have ruled out the kind of access to government provided by the British Labour Party. There have been links between the trade union confederations and political parties but they have not given the trade unions a great deal of influence in parliament and government. The closest link since the Second World War has been the one between the Communist Party and the CGT. After the beginning of the Cold War and the exclusion of the communist ministers from the government in 1947, there was a long period during which the Communist Party was politically isolated. Other parties refused to cooperate with it and this condemned the party to a role of almost sterile opposition. The CGT, therefore, did not have very effective parliamentary representation and it had no direct political access to the government. The Communist Party has recently been emerging from its long isolation and the conclusion, in June 1972, of a pact between the socialists and the communists may bring important changes in the relations between trade unions and political parties. If a very close-knit coalition of the Left was successful in elections this would provide a rallying point for all the main trade union confederations. It would also allow the CGT to loosen its connection with Communist tactics and doctrine which some sections of the membership increasingly favour.

The smaller confederations have been rather better served by their parliamentary associates. The CGT-FO had allies in the Socialist Party and the CFTC in the *Mouvement*

Républicain Populaire. The links were informal and tended to weaken as time passed. The honeymoon period between CFTC and the MRP after the Second World War was over by the early 1950s when the more militant leaders of the CFTC came to regard the MRP as too conservative for their taste. There were leading members of the MRP such as Henri Meck and Théo Braun, who were very much identified with the trade unions right until the moment, in 1966, when the MRP went out of existence, but they were not the dominant element in the party. The issue which split the CGT in 1947 on whether to approve of Marshall aid won for the minority, who set up the CGT-FO, the immediate sympathy of the Socialist Party. There were and continued to be many personal connections between the SFIO and the CGT-FO but both sides were concerned to maintain their distance. The trade unionists, having experienced communist interference in trade union affairs, were not disposed to encourage close ties with any political party. The socialists did not want to be allied with a trade union confederation because they considered that this would be a constraint on their parliamentary and governmental activities.

Under the Fourth Republic, the trade unions had, overall, a reasonable amount of parliamentary influence with three large parties of which two, the MRP and the SFIO, were important parties in government, representing their interests and providing channels of information. Moreover, the nature of the political system made it difficult for governments to administer policies which would do positive damage to the trade unions. Any reasonably well organized pressure group in a system of weak party discipline and unstable governments could, if not impose its wishes on the government, at least veto legislation to which it strongly objected. The system changed in very important respects after De Gaulle returned to power in 1958. Ministerial instability disappeared, and from 1962 the Gaullist parties had an absolute majority in the National Assembly. The participation in government of parties friendly towards trade unions came to an end; the Gaullist members of Parliament have little contact and sympathy with the trade union movement.

At the beginning of the Fifth Republic the government, led by De Gaulle and Debré, was determined to reassert the authority of the state which it considered had been undermined by the claims of sectional interests and the activities of pressure groups. There was nothing like a systematic anti-trade-union policy on the part of the government but some actions were taken which the trade unions disapproved. The government reduced the influence of important committees on which trade unions were represented, such as the *comités techniques paritaires* and the boards of the nationalized industries. Despite the opposition of the unions the Strikes (Early Warning) Bill was passed in 1963 and a number of executive decisions taken to limit the rights of unions representing public employees. On the other hand, De Gaulle and his ministers encouraged some forms of functional representation and took, for example, more notice of the Economic and Social Council than their predecessors. The reduction of the influence of Parliament has tended to increase, in some cases, the amount of direct contact between the government and important interest groups. This has been especially to the liking of the CGT leadership. Although the Fifth Republic has in general been more authoritative than the previous regime in its dealings with interest groups, the government has not had everything its own way in its relations with the trade unions. Because it has been much more consistently concerned about the level of wage settlements it has tended to become involved in trying to settle major strikes at a fairly early stage. This exposes it to the possibility of defeat if there is sufficient determination on the part of the workers and if they have a high degree of public sympathy. The government has been able to engage in what amounts to strike-breaking when it has used army trucks to carry passengers during strikes of Paris transport workers. These strikes are very unpopular with the public, but when the coalminers went on strike in 1963 they received support from a wide range of groups, including Catholic clergy and even some employers. This sympathy and the strikers' militancy brought about a defeat for the government in a major confrontation, causing De Gaulle's personal popularity to fall to its lowest point whilst he was in office.

The 'Events' of May-June 1968

Although the strikes that followed the revolt of the university students in 1968 were not as widespread as was believed at the time, they were unique in French labour history, both in form and extent. The country was paralysed by the closing down of all the major manufacturing concerns and transport facilities for a fortnight — in many cases much longer — and the occupation of a large number of factories. Factories had been occupied in the great wave of strikes in 1936, but an important motive at that time was to prevent the use of strike-breakers. In 1968 the occupations were partly imitative (the students had taken over the universities), partly to revive the enthusiasm of the great days of the Popular Front and partly to help maintain solidarity among the workers. The atmosphere in the factories was usually more down to earth than the imaginative romanticism found in the universities, but there was something approaching a revolutionary climate of opinion.

The leaders of the French Communist Party and all the main trade union leaders were convinced that there was not a revolutionary situation because the government was capable of defending itself if physically attacked. The overwhelming Gaullist victory in the elections of June 1968 showed that they were right in their assessment that revolutionary change, and violence in the streets, were very unpopular with the majority of the French electorate. The views of the communist and trade union leaders were not, however, universally shared by the rank and file of their membership. The union leaders quickly got down to negotiations with the employers and the government in very unstable and uncertain circumstances. The government looked as though it might fall, the employers were helpless and could not even gain access to their factories, and relations between union leaders and union members were often distant and hostile. The militants accused the trade union leaders of being weak and ill-suited to promote working-class aspirations. They charged them with being 'bureaucratic', an allegation made against almost all established institutions in 1968. At first sight the charge appears ludicrous when applied to the trade unions. They lacked funds, had relatively few permanent officials and their discipline was weak. The substance of the charge was not, however, that the unions had rigid and unwieldly hierarchies but that the leaders were out of touch with the grass roots. The demand for working-class unity, frequently made in 1968, was often an expression of hostility towards the existing unions, divided among themselves, according to their critics, by political considerations far removed from the shop-floor.

However it is possible, with hindsight, to regard the events, from the unions' point of view, as a fairly conventional sort of crisis. Their relations with the government in the period leading up to 1968 were poor because of its authoritarian manner. The unions were particularly upset by the reform of the social security system in 1967, pushed through with minimal consultation. They were also feeling relatively weak and lacking in bargaining power because a small industrial recession at the beginning of 1968 had slowed down salary increases and increased unemployment. Frustrations were building up and the government and the employers did not seem in a mood to make concessions easily. The strikes of 1968 started at the grass roots level and were then taken over by the federations and confederations which negotiated on the strikers' behalf. This chain of events has occurred fairly frequently in the past, and in this respect May 1968 was not unusual.

The aftermath of the 'events'

The agreements that settled the crisis contained nothing new; all the concessions had been claimed before, sometimes years before, the events of May 1968. The main provisions of the 'accords de Grenelle' were a straightforward pay rise of 10 per cent across the board and an increase of a third in the national minimum wage (SMIG). The CFDT and the CGT-FO had previously demanded that there should be a reduction of the differential in wage rates between trades and between Paris and the provinces. The generalization of some types of bonus payment, the drastic increase in SMIG and other more detailed measures helped towards these ends. The place of trade unions inside the factories had long been a bone of contention, with many employers tenaciously resisting incursions by the unions into the firms' time and premises. A law of December 1968 satisfied the unions' long-standing demand to have right of access to places of employment and to do business during working hours. An important agreement on employment eventually reached in February 1969 was hailed as a great step forward, but the main lines were suggested by the then Prime Minister, Georges Pompidou, as long ago as July 1967. A great social crisis had apparently done little more than hurry along negotiations on previously formulated demands, thus confirming the rather cynical view that in France a revolution is required to obtain a few reforms.

Of the three main confederations, the CFDT was apparently most affected by the events. In general it became more left-wing and began to adopt the language of the class war. But under a revolutionary vocabulary, the old gradualist position was reformulated. The objectives of *autogestion* (literally, self-management), democratic planning of the economy and the socialization of the means of production will, according to the official CFDT doctrine, be reached slowly by workers acquiring more and more information, participating in committees of government and in private industry, and by limiting the power of the employers to take independent decisions by action at the plant level. Although the aim was a complete transformation of society, this would be achieved not by sudden and violent revolution but by education and painstaking negotiations at all levels. The new left-wing elements attracted to the CFDT during and immediately after May 1968 were not in favour of this gradualist approach: tension between *gauchistes* and the orthodox within the CFDT led to considerable turmoil within the confederation.

Not surprisingly, the CGT-FO was overwhelmed by the events of May 1968 and had no united response to them. Some sections adopted revolutionary attitudes and broke agreements on unity of action with the CGT because they considered that the communist-led unions were being too cautious. In other places new CGT-FO *syndicats* were established by those who objected to the occupation of the factories and the harassment of non-strikers. The balance of opinion within the confederation was in favour of moderation. Although still claiming to be faithful to the Charter of Amiens, the CGT-FO has never been a revolutionary force. The one aspect of the Charter which still has a place in the attitudes of the confederation is the desire to keep the state and political parties out of industrial conflicts. This prejudice and the divisions among its members seemed grave handicaps in the circumstances of 1968, but ably led by its general secretary, André Bergeron, the CGT-FO was an influential negotiator in the agreements that followed the crisis. The events revealed in a dramatic way the extreme diversity of views within the confederation; it was, and remains, a rather ramshackle coalition whose only common denominator is deeply felt anti-communism.

The CGT remained true to its past and to its doctrines during and after the events of 1968 and refused to accept that they called for a reconsideration of the nature and strategy of trade unions. The Maoists, Trotskyites and other extreme left-wing groups bitterly attacked the CGT and the Communist Party, holding them responsible for preventing a proletarian revolution. The critics allege that the confederation and the party have become reformists but the doctrine of the CGT remains the same. In specific demands the CGT remains conservative in some respects, favouring lower taxes and the maintenance of wage differentials, to avoid impairing the unity of the working class by alienating any groups of workers. The confederation is unwilling to accept agreements for fixed periods of time, particularly if they involve commitments not to strike. Its intention is to create the feeling that conflict is permanent and to allow it to take advantage of discontents as they arise. Its leaders have reaffirmed that their task is not to make the existing order more just and equitable but to prepare the way for its destruction by encouraging a high level of class consciousness and combativity. Whether or not this has become empty rhetoric is a matter about which there are strongly conflicting views, but it is clear that fewer and fewer Frenchmen believe in the seriousness of the CGT's revolutionary intentions.

The present position and prospects

The three main trade union confederations survived the upheaval of May-June 1968, and, with some modifications, have preserved their distinctive character. But since that time there has been a greater degree of disarray in the unions: 'contestation' by minorities within the confederations, largely directed at their own leadership, and wild cat strikes have been on the increase. Although many of the old trade-union leaders regarded the attitudes expressed during the crisis as 'revolutionary infantilism', the aspirations raised had to be taken into account. May 1968 undoubtedly stimulated self-criticism and raised the level, as well as the temperature, of debate within the unions. But after the excitement of the crisis a certain lassitude set in and there was something of a reversion to old positions. For example, when in 1970 the CGT published a document 'Thèmes de réflexion sur les perspectives du socialisme pour la France et le rôle des syndicats', the newly elected general secretary of the CFDT, Edmond Marie, issued a cautious response, expressing reservations about the 'poussée unitaire sentimentale' and saying that there were important differences between the confederations. The grass roots sentiment in favour of working-class unity has been a stimulus towards new agreements between the confederations such as that concluded between the CFDT and CGT in December 1970 on pensions and trade union liberties. But these agreements are of a traditional type and no great progress has been made towards a greater degree of organizational unity.

In the arena of electoral politics, the old divisions persist. For the parliamentary elections of 1973, the CGT recommended voting for communist candidates, the CFDT for the Union of the Left (either communist or socialist candidates) and the CGT-FO remained officially neutral. The membership fragmented even further and, according to a contemporary public opinion poll, working-class voting behaviour expressed as a percentage of union membership was as follows:

Union membership	Extreme Left	Communist	Socialist	Reformers	Gaullist coalition	Other Right
CGT	1	58	29	3	6	3
CFDT	11	21	30	6	27	5
CGT-FO	3	20	43	5	23	6
Other union	4	21	23	16	31	5
Non-union	4	23	20	14	36	3

François Mitterand, the candidate of the Union of the Left for the Presidency of the Republic in 1974, attracted almost unanimous support from the unions, and the great majority of union members voted for him. The circumstances of presidential elections by universal suffrage are peculiar in that they compel a polarization of opinion into two camps. The general agreement manifest in the elections of 1974 is very unlikely to lead to a united left-wing political movement closely associated with the trade union movement in the foreseeable future.

The event in the present decade which stimulated for a time the most hope and discussion within the trade union movement had little to do with parties and elections. In 1973 the bankruptcy of the Swiss-owned watch making firm at Besançon, Lip, led to the occupation of the factory by the workers, nationwide agitation and the eventual establishment of a workers' cooperative. After many vicissitudes the experiment eventually collapsed in 1976 despite the injection of government money and management expertise. Revolutionary hopes were again re-kindled by the audacity of the Lip workers and again the unions were typically divided in their attitude. The CGT was very cautious and the national (as opposed to the local) leadership tended to the view that workers' control of enterprises under the capitalist order were bound to fail. The CFDT enthusiasts considered that capitalism would be abolished by the route taken at Lip.

The debates and discontents in the unions have revived interest in the evolution of the working class among politicians, planners, journalists and sociologists. The implications of technological and social change on working-class attitudes and behaviour were subjects of discussion before 1968, in such books as Serge Mallet's *La Nouvelle classe ouvrière*, published in 1963. After 1968, the changes are generally recognized to have important implications not only for trade union organization but also for the Communist Party, the new coalition of the left-wing parties and for the nature of the political system as a whole. No common view has emerged about the processes of change because the values of each observer tend to colour the conclusions which they reach. There is, however, no sign that large sections of the working class are about to abandon, in the immediate future, their traditional taste for revolutionary ideology coupled with reformist practice, punctuated from time to time by violent protest.

Bibliography

Adam, P., Bon, F., Capdevielle, J. and Mouriaux, R., *L'Ouvrier français en 1970*. Paris, Colin, 1970. The results of a detailed opinion survey, administered to a sample of over 1000 workers. An essential work for the understanding of working-class attitudes and values.

Andrieux, A. and Lignon, J., *Le Militant syndicaliste d'aujourd'hui*. Paris, Denoël, 1973. The report of a survey about how militants became involved in trade union action and about their attitudes and motivations.

Bauchard, P. and Bruzek, M., *Le Syndicalisme à l'epreuve*. Paris, Laffont, 1968. The reporting of the effects of May-June 1968 written immediately after the events by two skilful reporters.

Lefranc, G., *Le Syndicalisme en France*. Paris, PUF, 1968. A brief introduction to the trade union movement, written by the most prolific author on this subject, giving an excellent historical perspective.

Lefranc, G. *Le Mouvement syndical de la Libération aux évènements de mai-juin 1968*. Paris, Payot, 1969. The best account of the post-war history of the trade union movement, although written in a way that assumes a good deal of knowledge of the subject.

Mallet, S., *La Nouvelle classe ouvrière*. Paris, Seuil, 1963. The book that opened a wide ranging debate in the 1960s on the effect of technological change and prosperity on the working class.

Reynaud, J.D., *Les Syndicats en France*, 2 vols. Paris, Colin, 1975 (second edition). An introductory textbook which gives a comprehensive coverage of the subject with a useful bibliography and excerpts from important documents in trade union history.

The most useful trade union journals are: *Force Ouvrière* (CGT-FO), *Le Peuple* (CGT), *Syndicalisme* (CFTC-CFDT), *Vie Ouvrière* (CGT), *Le Creuset-Voix des Cadres* (CGT). At a more scholarly level there are *Etudes Sociales et Syndicales*, *Sociologue du Travail*.

4 Foreign policy

Alan Clark

Introduction

The significance of a country's foreign policy is normally greater than the general interest which it commands within that country. France supplies no exception to this observation, yet to the outsider some knowledge of its foreign policy is helpful, not merely to understand France's situation in the world, or even its internal condition (the two are often inextricably mixed), but in order to appreciate better the specifically French view (or views) of its own national condition: the French self-image at a given time, justifiable or not, laudable or derisory. Involving as it does a host of general and sectional interests, recent French foreign policy has provoked in Frenchmen and foreigners alike a great variety of interpretations, many of them passionate.

The Gaullist heritage

The essential principles of De Gaulle's foreign policy in the 1960s were few and uncomplicated. The vital initial postulate was the paramount importance of national independence, the re-establishment of which would enable France to regain its previous, traditional position of international eminence. In independence France would be free to enter into multiform cooperation with other nations and thus fulfil its historical 'vocation' of the promotion of peace and of certain civilized values. On the other hand without independence valid international cooperation would not be possible since it would inevitably involve the subordination of one of the cooperating partners; national indignity apart, such cooperation-in-subordination would in practice be bound to fail.

From 1958 French foreign policy quickly became 'le domaine réservé' of the President of the Republic who accorded it prime importance, determining its major orientations and deciding particular, often crucial issues. Although the effective contributions of his Prime Ministers and his Minister of Foreign Affairs have been insufficiently acknowledged, De Gaulle did conduct a personal policy in an individual fashion. It has been suggested that his foreign policy was characterized more by the originality of its diplomatic style than by the solidity of its achievements and it is as well to distinguish the two aspects. Yet, substantial or more intangible, important changes in French foreign policy certainly did take place under De Gaulle. Following the broadly successful and relatively rapid decolonization of France's African possessions and the settlement of the Algerian War, De Gaulle had worked to establish national independence on the only basis that, in his mind, was valid: French control of an effective national security system. This led him in 1966 to withdraw France from the integrated military command of a NATO dominated by the USA, and to develop a French nuclear strategy and strike capacity. As the converse of this disengagement from the American orbit, a policy of cooperation and détente with the USSR and the 'satellite' countries of Eastern Europe was pursued with enthusiasm. In European affairs, French intransigence concerning the establishment in the EEC of a common agricultural policy, successful though it proved to be, took second place in De Gaulle's estimation, behind his political ambition to establish a confederal association of West European states, a 'Europe of nations' in which France would resume its historical position of leader. Between and distinct from the super-powers of East and West, De Gaulle's Western Europe was to have been indispensable to world stability — 'la condition indispensable de l'équilibre du monde'. But after his best efforts (the Fouchet Plans, 1961-2, and the Franco-German treaty, 1963) had failed to impress the Community partners, his political Europeanism was of necessity reduced to an unshakeable opposition to any proposals which might lead to the emergence of a supranationalist Europe, more or less aligned with the USA. Fear of such an 'Atlanticization' of

Europe was prominent among the reasons for French opposition to British membership of the Community. Often preached in the UN, the gaullist gospel of the independence of nation-states was received with appreciation in many parts of the Third World; France's international standing was enhanced still further by the vigorous — and generous — cooperation policies it pursued, particularly in the newly independent African francophone states. Nevertheless the function of arbiter in international conflicts which De Gaulle had on occasion loudly assigned to a 'neutral' France was losing credibility at least with Israel as, in the Middle East, French sympathies lay increasingly with the Arab oil-supplying countries (1967 arms embargo).

For Couve de Murville (Minister of Foreign Affairs, 1958-1968) De Gaulle was beyond doubt 'un homme d'une passion intransigeante et sa passion était la France'; his foreign policy invariably pursued 'l'intérêt national au sens le plus élevé du terme'. Couve de Murville was — still is — a prominent cultivator of the gaullist mystique and his assessment should not be accepted uncritically. Both within and outside France numerous critics have accused the foreign policy of De Gaulle of being anachronistic, unrealistic and therefore dangerous, merely negative, or — perhaps most damning — of being the product of an old man's idiosyncrasies. In principle at least the pursuit of national independence by De Gaulle was never a matter of ignoring or underestimating harsh world realities; rather he constantly affirmed the priority of the national reality as the vital precondition of international dealings. His basic position was not of necessity nationalist in the pejorative sense of that word (although many foreign commentators saw it as such) to the extent that France's 'nationalness' sought peaceful rather than aggressive relations with other nations. It could be held of course that, unlike Louis XIV, De Gaulle had little real choice in the matter.

Foreign policy under Pompidou (1969-1974)

It is certain that at De Gaulle's resignation (April 1969), French prestige stood higher than at any time since 1940 and, arguably, since before the First World War. During the 1960s France had exerted a determining — not everyone would say beneficient — influence on the economic and political evolution of Europe and of a large portion of Africa, and the voice of France had been heard — if not always listened to — in far wider fields, from Washington to Moscow and in the many capitals of the Third World. Foreign reaction to the new French standing in the world was doubtless an unstable amalgam of resentment and respect, envy and affection. Apart from predictable reservations concerning the expense involved in maintaining De Gaulle's nuclear programme and cooperation policies, domestic French feelings were still in the main ones of sympathy and gratitude for a needed restoration of national dignity (which is not to underestimate the groundswell of discontent at social and economic problems manifested in the events of May-June 1968). That the principles and personality of the president himself had been vital to this restoration was no less clear, in particular to those many gaullists who were determined to ensure France's continued fidelity to the pattern laid down since 1958. In true French fashion, De Gaulle's death in 1970 only intensified (in some cases, almost sanctified) that determination.

To succeed so exceptional a character as De Gaulle would have been a politically delicate affair in any circumstances. For reasons of temperament, experience and conviction Pompidou (De Gaulle's Prime Minister between 1962 and 1968) was well qualified to appreciate how mixed a blessing his gaullist inheritance was. Pompidou's political style tended to be pragmatic, prudent, closer to a traditional conservatism than that of his predecessor: a more moderate tone was inevitable, but ran the risk of appearing mediocre, too ready for compromise. Moreover Pompidou's political experience (he had been particularly prominent in handling the strikes and demonstrations of 1968, at a time when De Gaulle's control of things seemed to falter) had bred in him a consciousness of the pressing need to accelerate the modernization of French industry and to maintain economic growth. And not only for internal political reasons, but in order to ensure the economic strength on which the perpetuation of a gaullist foreign policy depended — a condition which the more loftily conceived ideology of De Gaulle had been inclined to forget. While showing little sign of wanting to depart from the main lines of gaullist doctrine, pompidolean foreign policy did have its points of difference, born of an acknowledgement that circumstances had changed: two years after his election, Pompidou had effectively accepted the entry of Britain into the EEC. On the other hand the control of foreign policy remained, as in De Gaulle's day, firmly in the control of the new President of the Republic; indeed to the extent that it was informed by a greater awareness of France's internal economic needs and of the increasing integration of domestic and foreign interests, that control may be said to have intensified under Pompidou. Michel Jobert makes a useful distinction between *la vision* of De Gaulle's approach to foreign policy and *la gestion* of Pompidou's.

On at least two occasions in 1970 Pompidou reaffirmed France's determination to remain — in a spirit of independence — a member of the Atlantic Alliance; France would not however be rejoining the integrated defence structure of NATO. In defence policy Pompidou was faithful to the line of De Gaulle, maintaining the quiet modifications from the high rigidity of France's 1966 position that had been perceptible from 1968, but did not engage himself in any positive developments of that line. The cost of the nuclear arms programme began to weigh more heavily, both financially and politically. France's neglected conventional forces were by the early 1970s badly in need of modern equipment, and several embarrassing delays in the realization of stages in the nuclear programme had to be announced — to a public no longer enthralled by the general's rhetoric and more concerned to see increases in social spending. Criticism of the tiny size and doubtful efficacy of *la force de frappe* flourished: in the middle of Pompidou's presidency, France had progressed to the point where 9 out of a projected 18 ground-to-ground missiles stood ready in their silos in Haute-Provence, while 2 of a proposed fleet of 5 missile-firing nuclear submarines were in service by the end of 1972. Nevertheless France went ahead with its series of atmospheric nuclear tests in the Pacific with sufficient determination to resist the campaign of international protest led in 1973 by the governments of Australia and New Zealand. A truly gaullist president had no choice in the matter in any case. France had not signed the 1963 and 1968 international treaties related to nuclear disarmament and arms control and the agreement on the prevention of nuclear war signed between the USA and the USSR in June 1973 justified in Pompidou's eyes the earlier intransigence of De Gaulle. For France the June treaty was tantamount to the self-promotion of the two super-powers to the shared office of nuclear policeman for the rest of the world. It was a 'condominium' (the term was employed by the French Foreign Minister of the time, Jobert — a less diplomatic alternative would be a 'carve-up') which should not be confused with genuine progress towards international détente. For the French, the proof of the validity of their interpretation was seen in the joint and exclusive regulation of the October War in the Middle East (1973) by the USA and the USSR; the super-powers had decided to settle world affairs without consulting their allies. The final twelve months of his presidency amply underlined Pompidou's determined fidelity to basic gaullist principles relating to national security. At the Helsinki conference on European security and defence (July 1973) France solidly plugged the line of *national* responsibility for defence matters: merely because they had decided between themselves to become partners in world domination, after having been rivals for it, was no reason for the super-powers to be permitted to run European security as they wished. The blocs were again threatening French, and European, independence. Seen in this perspective, the gaullist nuclear capacity appeared more vital than ever. Speaking before the French National Assembly in October 1973 Jobert forecast the necessity in the longer term of ensuring the defensive autonomy of Europe; put in another way, this could be seen as a recall to De Gaulle's ideal of independence from the USA.

Pompidou's relations with the super-powers were not always as difficult as they became in 1973 and were at no stage sharply marked by the temperamental anti-Americanism to which many considered De Gaulle had on occasion succumbed. Prolonging the measure of cordiality established in early 1969 between De Gaulle and Nixon, Pompidou chose the USA for his first official overseas trip as President (January 1970). It was not an auspicious beginning: the visit was marred by American-Jewish demonstrations at French policy in the Middle East that apparently so enraged Pompidou that neutral territory was chosen for two later Franco-American summits in which he participated! Nevertheless some measure of agreement with regard to international monetary problems was reached at the Azores meeting with Nixon (December 1971) and the devaluation of the American dollar was announced jointly by the two leaders. Relations deteriorated considerably in 1973 when, as well as the USA-USSR treaty on the prevention of nuclear war, two major areas of discord emerged. In April the American Secretary of State, Kissinger, began a diplomatic campaign intended to ensure agreement between the USA and Europe as the latter proceeded more or less slowly towards economic and political union. There was talk in June of Kissinger proposing a 'new Atlantic charter' designed to promote this Atlanticist orientation of Europe. For the USA and for France's European partners the project had its merits: quite apart from its substantial economic interests in Western Europe, the USA ensured the lion's share of a NATO defensive system which sooner or later would be affected by the decisions of any politically united Europe of the future. But for France it was yet another attempt by the Americans to dominate, and this time not only the sovereignty of France but also the autonomy of a possible union of Europe were threatened. French resistance to American proposals for joint Western policies was underlined again at the end of 1973 when Pompidou rejected Kissinger's idea of forming a common front of oil importers for concerted action in response to the massive increases in the price of oil introduced by the exporting countries (October 1973). At the Washington energy conference (February 1974), French resistance to what Jobert regarded as the economic imperialism of the USA was made clear; France held out for a joint conference, to include the oil producers and in particular the Arab states. At the end of Pompidou's presidency (he died 2 April 1974) France appeared again in the familiar gaullist stance of isolated opposition to American intentions in several fields. And the defiance shown towards the allied super-power by the Pompidou-Jobert team, like that which De Gaulle had exhibited, was sympathetically received by French opinion.

Pompidou had all the more reason to continue to develop political links with the USSR in the context of gaullist 'balanced' relations with the super-powers as West Germany's *Ostpolitik*, long recommended by De Gaulle in the 1960s, was meeting with more success, both diplomatic and commercial, than was perhaps good for French interests. Until 1973, Pompidou's exchanges with Brezhnev were cordial and progress was made in Franco-Russian commercial and technical exchanges (there was room for it: in 1970 just 2 per cent of French exports went to the USSR). By contrast détente with other countries in Eastern Europe, so loudly hailed by the general, was maintained in little more than form — state visits (Tito came to Paris in 1970) and minor trade agreements. The treaty of June 1973 and the October War demonstrated again that in matters of real importance the USSR preferred to leave France out of account and treat directly with its American rival-partner. One notable consequence of the French position with regard to the super-powers was that, on his visit to Peking (September 1973) Pompidou found himself talking the same diplomatic language as the Chinese leaders: both disapproved of the 'collusion' between the USA and the USSR. For Pompidou their joint 'imperialism' was no less potentially dangerous than had been the conflict between the two blocs in the 1950s and 1960s.

Europe offered the greatest opportunity to Pompidou for creative departures in foreign policy. And innovation was needed. De Gaulle's intransigence had had much to do with the stagnant state in the late 1960s of both the EEC and the movement towards political union. Pompidou's general desire to set Europe in motion again was evident: a partisan of British entry since 1962, he reaffirmed his approval in principle of a widening of the EEC both during his election campaign and in an early presidential press-conference (July 1969). The European summit held at the Hague (December 1969) agreed to the opening of negotiations with candidate countries, notably Britain. Pompidou's positive contribution at The Hague, which represented a considerable change from De Gaulle's approach to European policy, was motivated by three principal considerations. Firstly, France's isolated position within the EEC could not be allowed to persist indefinitely and a prominent role in the re-launching of Europe would ensure French reintegration. Secondly the entry of Britain, financially troubled though it was, would contribute to an increase in the economic power of the EEC that was imperative if the pessimism then current in Brussels and Paris concerning the future viability of the Community was not to be proved justified. Finally, Pompidou probably looked to an integrated Britain to act with France to counterbalance within Europe the potentially menacing economic strength (and, therefore, political weight) of West Germany. Not that Pompidou offered Britain easy access to the Community. During the sometimes difficult negotiations (which began in June 1970) the familiar game of 'France v. the Five-plus-Britain' was replayed more than once, with French conditions centring on the financing of the common agricultural policy, a reinforcement of the administrative structures of the Community (in order to cope with the stresses that would be imposed by the expansion from 6 to 9 members) and a broadening of the Europeanization process (in legal, technical, scientific and other fields) with a view to facilitating political union. French opinion was not particularly enthusiastic and the British public clearly divided on the matter of entry but, in a fashion reminiscent of De Gaulle's personalized intervention in major policy orientations, the essentials appear to have been agreed on in the Paris meeting between Pompidou and Heath (20-21 May 1971). A month later it was agreed in Luxembourg that Britain should enter the EEC on 1 January 1973.

The entry of Britain (and Ireland and Denmark) into the EEC was not of itself likely to answer growing criticism of the inefficiency of European institutions and the imperfections of the Common Market's policies. In particular in 1971 a unified monetary policy was as desirable as it appeared unlikely. The bulk of Pompidou's activity from this time was given to the promotion of greater European union, especially in the monetary and political spheres. His efforts suffered a demoralizing political set-back from the relative failure of a referendum he held (April 1972) on the enlargement of Europe: 40 per cent abstentions (the highest rate since Napoleon!) were recorded and only 36 per cent of the electorate voted 'Yes'. It was an attempt at the grand gaullist gesture that went wrong: he had not received the clear popular mandate he had hoped for and the French hand at the autumn summit had not been strengthened in advance. Called at Pompidou's suggestion, the meeting of the Nine in Paris (October 1972) established a calendar for a political union that was to be achieved by 1980. Pompidou did not depart from De Gaulle's insistence on a confederal union of states, although he was more sensitive to the isolation of France that was liable to result if that policy was presented in too absolute a fashion. His preference was for progressive, concrete realizations (although his suggestion that a European political secretariat be formed met with little response). Little hard agreement was reached at Paris, if goodwill was available in plenty, and the total disarray of European opinion on monetary problems remained. Pompidou's initiative also led to the exceptional meeting of the nine European heads of government in Copenhagen (December 1973). Held in the turbulent aftermath of the oil crisis, it was a disappointing summit that served to add energy and raw materials policies to the sum of Europe's disagreements — and to underscore a re-emergence of French isolation within the Community.

Pompidou's efforts to improve political cooperation appeared to have counted for little, as with Britain and Germany in particular looking sympathetically at American initiatives (Kissinger's 'new Atlantic charter' and his policy of a common front of oil-importing countries), France was left alone to plug the old gaullist line of national independence and resistance to the 'hegemony' of the USA. But would such a policy, useful as it might have been in the 1960s, prove appropriate in the wider and more complex Europe of the 1970s and 1980s? France was no longer economically independent of the rest of the Common Market: in 1972, approximately 25 per cent of French exports were made to West Germany while another 25 per cent went to the other EEC countries. The degree of dependence will only increase with the growth of the Community. In these circumstances was old-style gaullist absolutism on national sovereignty still defensible, or even possible? In April 1974 it was not certain how long France would be able to continue to pay the price of its claimed independence. If the bill were to prove too high, the only alternative appeared to be an Atlantic Europe, that is one whose political, economic and monetary evolution would be realigned according to the directives of the USA. And that would mean the end of gaullist Europe.

Not without alienating important sections of French informed opinion, Pompidou remained firm in the pro-Arab stance adopted by De Gaulle in 1967, and conducted his Middle East policy with a sure sense of national economic interests. The diplomatic position remained much as before (guarantees for both Israel and the Palestinian people and a negotiated settlement based on mutual concessions), but France's energy supplies were also involved — supplies which it was quite vital to protect in the period leading to the oil crisis of late 1973. Pompidou's pragmatism became glaringly evident when, while maintaining the embargo on arms to Israel, he agreed that France should supply Libya with 100 Mirages (January 1970). Gaullist claims to impartiality in the Middle East fell to pieces: Pompidou's France was no longer a peacemaker but an influence-exerter and a cultivator of interests. French diplomats covered the Middle Eastern states thoroughly in the context of a long-term policy intended to develop French industrial, commercial and cultural interests in the area.

Pompidou's action in the Middle East should be seen within his wider policy of expanding France's role in the Mediterranean. By emphasizing southern interests Pompidou thought France could rebalance the northern predominance that would result from an expanded Europe, and regain some of its lost importance by occupying a prominent position in the 'new' Mediterranean that might emerge. Efforts were made to implement the scheme from 1969 and met with moderate success. By mid-1970 France had developed closer contacts with Lisbon and Madrid; a military agreement was signed with the latter, to which 30 Mirages were sold. French determination to improve relations with the Maghreb also showed results and after the storms of the 1960s diplomatic normality was restored between France and Morocco in 1969. Algeria posed a more important and more difficult problem. The loss of French oil concessions in the Algerian nationalizations of 1971 was a heavy blow to accept as, with economic following political decolonization during the 1960s, France had witnessed the erosion of the privileged exchanges with Algeria which in 1962 De Gaulle had anticipated. The situation between the two countries was sometimes delicate: French imports of Algerian wine were stopped in 1970, the proportion of French aid going to Algeria dropped steadily and, following racial tension in Marseilles, Algeria suspended the heavy emigration of its workers to France (September 1973). But, in spite of the fact that the commercial exchanges firmly favoured Algeria, Pompidou persisted in his efforts to cultivate good relations, looking to France's longer-term economic and strategic interests. His concept of an Arabo-Latin Mediterranean was farsighted and perhaps realistic, but it was also not without its opportunism (at the expense of Israel) and somehow lacked the cachet of his predecessor's more loftily conceived diplomacy. It was a policy defensible as prudent manoeuvring, but one which also contained the implicit admission that France's role, after being played on the world stage, would in future be effectively limited to Western Europe and the Mediterranean. And a presence in Africa.

While President, Pompidou visited at least once most of the former French territories in Black Africa; after 1958 De Gaulle did not venture beyond the countries of the Maghreb. The difference illustrates Pompidou's greater concern for a cooperation policy that was less paternalistic, more open to the rapidly changing circumstances of the Third World. Wherever possible the privileged relations between France and its former colonies were maintained, but Pompidou agreed readily enough to African demands for liberalizing reforms of the 1960 cooperation agreements. Although it actually increased in volume, the proportion of the French budget given to cooperation declined to 1974; aid from the private sector (banks, industry, etc.,) became almost as important as public aid — and less disinterested. Further, the French cooperation programme began to spread its funds and expertise beyond its traditional African spheres of influence: in 1970 40 per cent of French aid went to developing countries outside *le zone franc*. Against this, critics could point to the fact that one-fifth of all French aid went to the DOM-TOM. Nevertheless Pompidou's modified maintenance of France's relatively good cooperation record demanded a degree of political courage at a time when such expensive policies, no longer buoyed up by De Gaulle's charisma, attracted diminishing public support. It is clear that particularly as the oil crisis deepened Pompidou saw the problems of the Third World (the stability of prices received for raw materials, financial relations with the developed world) in global, long-term perspectives and, by 1974, the familiar gaullist thesis of an international mediatory role for France had cropped up again. At the Washington energy conference and at the UN (April 1974), Jobert's refusal to follow the American 'common front' strategy on oil prices and his stress on the necessity for developing countries to be fully involved in all discussions relating to international trade were welcomed by the many countries of the Third World dependent on prices received for their exports to the West. Gaullist 'cultural nationalism' enjoyed mixed fortunes in the early 1970s. On the one hand hundreds of French primary and secondary teachers continued to work in Black Africa and the idea of *la francophonie* began to take on organizational form (for example, in 1969 29 countries including Canada participated in the Francophone Congress held in Niger); on the other hand, the French cultural presence in South America supposedly stimulated by De Gaulle's visit of 1964 had totally evaporated.

Foreign policy under Giscard d'Estaing (1974-   )

Since the election of Giscard d'Estaing (May 1974) the patterns of French foreign policy, while not breaking free from their gaullist mould, have in some aspects undergone modification and in others become confused and difficult to decipher. Nor is the lack of historical perspective entirely responsible for such lack of clarity. Change with continuity had been the unoriginal keynote of Giscard's election campaign and he promised change in the area of foreign policy when he addressed the French diplomatic corps in the month following his victory. He indicated three points of change. An extension of French involvement in international (presumably other than bilateral) cooperation with developing countries and a 'new era' of international relations based on 'le respect et l'estime mutuels, [et] un esprit de compréhension et de liberté' were promised. The form such change might adopt was not easy to imagine from the third point: while remaining independent in its commitments and decisions, '[la France] veut désormais consacrer ses forces, son imagination et son talent à forger son avenir'. A certain tone, of imprecise idealism infused to all appearances with boundless good-will, had been set. And yet a number of features of Giscard's reputation in the field of foreign policy were widely acknowledged at the start of his term of office. He was first and foremost a convinced European and looked to a politically united Europe having its own defence, currency and foreign policy. Although he has always denied it, critics (many gaullists, most socialists and all the communists) accused and still accuse him of Atlanticist leanings, of working for greater French and European association with the USA, in particular with regard to economic and defensive structures. By his own admission Giscard was more positively internationalist in his approach to foreign policy: problems now posed themselves on a world scale, state-to-state relations (à la De Gaulle) were no longer sufficient in many cases and what he termed *une politique mondiale* was vital, although national sovereignty was to be firmly preserved. Such a global perspective necessitated what Giscard constantly referred to in 1974 as a policy of *concertation* (the word is not found in the 1975 edition of *Le Petit Robert*, and says much for Giscard's attention to the modernity of his political image), that is of dialogue and harmonious coordination rather than intimidation and conflict (*la confrontation*). To what extent an implied criticism of De Gaulle's intransigent defence of (his version of) national interests was to be detected in these giscardian emphases was of course a matter of political opinion.

But elsewhere change was undeniable, not least in Giscard's political position. As leader of the Républicains Indépendents (IR) he was the first non-gaullist President of the Fifth Republic and while he chose a dynamic member of the UDR, Chirac, as his first Prime Minister, it was clear from the first that despite their internal divisions, the parliamentary gaullists would ensure that any departures from their founder's principles (in particular with regard to defence and national independence) did not pass uncriticized. It might have been thought that the narrowness of his electoral victory (less than 2 per cent more votes than Mitterrand, the candidate of the combined Left) would have restricted Giscard's freedom to conduct his own foreign policy — after all he could not claim the solid majority support on which the confidence of De Gaulle and Pompidou (until the 1972 referendum) had largely rested. Moreover the substantial gains made by the combined Left at the legislative elections of April 1973 have obliged Giscard to look to the centrist parties to provide the votes necessary for majorities which a diminished but critical UDR can no longer supply. The greater coherence of the parliamentary opposition has however yet to make a decisive impact in foreign policy matters: many observers consider that the brief final section of the Common Programme (signed in June 1972 by the PCF, PS and the left-wing radicals, and still in force) which outlines the foreign policy of a future French government of the Left is unimpressive and that, in the areas of defence and Europe in particular, it poses as many questions as it supplies answers.

Obliged to take account of a delicate political situation at home, Giscard came to power at a time of serious and persistent international difficulties. The oil crisis which had broken out in the Autumn of 1973 promised to involve other raw materials and threatened shaky international financial systems. Europe was in conflict, immobile if not actually regressive. The USA was in the final throes of Watergate (Nixon resigned August 1974). The new French President's large financial experience (Giscard had been a liberal Finance Minister under De Gaulle, 1962-6, and under Pompidou, 1969-74) was expected to produce in the conduct of foreign policy an intensification of pompidolean sensitivity to French economic interests. Complex and rapid change on all sides also encouraged a temperamentally willing Giscard to develop his predecessor's pragmatism: in a world characterized more by chaos than by order, *le pilotage à vue* and *la gestion de l'imprévisible* (the phrases are Giscard's) become the only practical attitude to adopt. Critics were not slow to ask what in such circumstances became of long-term strategy and basic principles. If the age in which De Gaulle's sharply defined foreign policy had flourished was long past Frenchmen of various political persuasions were not prepared to admit the fact and criticized Giscard according to criteria which were, explicitly or otherwise, gaullist. Couve de Murville did not perhaps exaggerate too much when he claimed, in December 1974, that 'tout est jugé maintenant dans le domaine de la politique étrangèrs par rapport à Charles de Gaulle'.

Even had he wanted to do otherwise Giscard would have been under pressure, for political and technological reasons, to adopt a defence policy acceptable to the UDR. Before election he promised to maintain and develop French nuclear weapons and guaranteed the absence of France from disarmament and non-proliferation talks which sought only to maintain the blocs of the super-powers. Yet even at this pre-presidential stage there were nuances which could have been interpreted as departures from pompidolean resolution. If nuclear tests at Muroroa must continue, only those which were *indispensable* would be held in the atmosphere (had 'gratuitous' tests been held previously?) and as soon as possible all future tests would be held underground. Giscard's accommodating attitude gained a measure of sympathy from those Pacific governments which had resented Pompidou's insensibility to their protests. Even underground, French tests have been fewer: 3 in 1975, 2 in 1976 (to mid-September). A further point worth noting in his election campaign was Giscard's optimism regarding the prospects for a European defence organization (one, that is, independent of American control), which, he thought, would come about 'plus vite qu'on ne le croit'. Pompidou would doubtless have considered such sentiments to be utopian.

Further modifications, often only of attitude, cropped up throughout 1974 after the presidential election. In October Giscard thought it necessary to make clear his idea of the strictly limited number of cases in which France's strategic nuclear forces might be employed: they would only be used dissuasively against other nuclear powers or against any power constituting a threat to French territory; he would never sanction their use, or even the threat of their use, against non-nuclear powers. Moderation, if only on the airless level of nuclear strategy. A mention (in June 1974) of the need to rationalize the budget of the nuclear development programme stirred doubts among some of the military hierarchy. Military cooperation between France and NATO was on the increase, although no official announcement had been made: the trend had begun, very quietly, under De Gaulle but in 1974-5 it was seen as symptomatic of the new president's desire for reconciliation with the USA. Integral gaullists and the PCF denounced an intended military reintegration of France within NATO, and therefore a betrayal of national independence to Washington, but with little more evidence than a sense of vagueness concerning exactly what defence policy Giscard *was* promoting. The tenth anniversary of De Gaulle's withdrawal decision of 1966 passed with virtually no demonstrable variation from the gaullist line. Indeed under Giscard the specific role of the French nuclear forces had been recognized within the Atlantic

Alliance (Brussels declaration, June 1974), a third generation of strategic weapons (multi-headed thermonuclear devices) had been brought to technical perfection and, faithful to Pompidou's intentions, the presence of the French fleet in the Mediterranean had been increased. The percentage of the national budget given to defence is scheduled to rise from 17.0 in 1976 to 20.0 in 1982.

In June 1976 an uneasy calm was shattered by the publication in the semi-official *Revue de défense nationale* of an article by General Méry, a senior French military strategist. Published with governmental approval, Méry's article constituted a redefinition of France's military links with the Atlantic Alliance. The fundamental basis of national independence was reasserted, but the importance of avoiding France's military isolation was also stressed: France should participate with its allies (in military exercises, etc.,) although not within the integrated system of NATO as at present organized. But Méry's concept of *la sanctuarisation élargie* and his acceptance of the possibility of France's participation in *la bataille de l'avant* (that is, on the eastern borders of West Germany) appeared to imply a dilution of dissuasion policy and an increased degree of French involvement in NATO's military structures. Finally Méry maintained that a European defensive system was impossible without the prior establishment of European political union, and even then he found it difficult to imagine such a system existing in total independence of the USA. The article was vulnerable to charges of admitting *rapprochement* between the defence strategies of France and NATO, a most un-gaullist movement. With shifting emphases Giscard, Chirac and Defence Minister Bourges assured all and sundry that national defence policy had not changed. The UDR was divided, the socialists were hostile, although for various reasons and to different degrees, while the communists were irreproachably united in their denunication of Giscard's supposed schemes — on the gaullist grounds of the paramount importance of national independence! Are French strategic policies undergoing covert change, or was the Méry affair a storm in a tea-cup, stirred up for political purposes? At the time of writing (September 1976) it was not possible to tell. What was sure was that for a clearly comprehensible, essentially single policy appeared to have been substituted a changing set of ambiguities.

Giscard's predicted determination to effect a *rapprochement* with the USA became evident in the months following his election and by early 1975 a more cordial tone in relations between Paris and Washington had been established. After the new Foreign Minister Sauvagnargues had been warmly received by Kissinger at Camp David (September 1974) the way lay open for a presidential summit. When Giscard met Ford in Martinique (December 1974) both sides were keen to stress the improvement in their relations (compared with the noisy clashes between Jobert and Kissinger, the change seemed real enough, if 'psychological' more than political) and appeared to reach a widely welcomed compromise position on the question of the composition of an international energy conference. This apparently successful plugging of a more moderate line did not however disarm Giscard's critics among the gaullists (for whom conciliation with the Americans would sooner or later involve a compromise with national independence and dignity) and on the Left (for whom, beyond considerations of national sovereignty, Giscard's *atlantisme* would lead to even greater French submission to American financial and industrial interests). Both considered their fears justified when (in January 1975) with the quiet dropping of the originally French idea of a trilateral energy conference Giscard appeared to have bowed to American pressure. If the line between useful conciliation and harmful compromise is difficult to draw, certainly the potential for clashes of interest between the two countries remained considerable. From Autumn 1974 French and American firms and governments competed fiercely for contracts for the replacement of several hundred F104 Starfighter aircraft of the European countries' NATO fleets. In a sense this was symptomatic of Franco-American relations under Giscard: albeit improved in tone they remained conflictual, but transformed from predominantly political into largely commercial terms.

Such at least was the state of play in 1976. Giscard's official visit to the USA (May 1976) was a public success: the sentimental ties between the two countries established at the time of the Revolution were duly celebrated, it was decided to work towards greater coordination of policies relating to the Middle East, southern Africa and the Third World, and Giscard assured Congress that France would continue to contribute to the efficacy of the Atlantic Alliance. Yet soon after the USA obliged South Korea to withdraw from a contract to purchase a nuclear power plant from France and in August 1976 Kissinger blatantly attempted to intervene in the sale by France to Pakistan of a uranium retreatment plant. Although the contract with Pakistan may be fulfilled, such 'interference' by the Americans was resented by the bulk of French political opinion and it will be interesting to see how long Giscard will be able to afford, politically and economically, to maintain his policy of conciliation.

As with the USA France's relations with the USSR since April 1974 have at times been characterized by a change in tone, although in this case the evolution has occurred more slowly and in the direction of doubt and uncertainty. During Giscard's first year of office Franco-Russian relations were pursued diligently and fruitfully: both Sauvagnargues (in Moscow, July 1974) then Giscard himself (on the occasion of Brezhnev's visit, December 1974) emphasized their determination to develop still further the policy of détente and cooperation initiated by De Gaulle and which had become established in the mid-1970s as a permanent feature of French foreign policy. Together with a general agreement on economic cooperation covering the period to 1980, substantial energy and industrial agreements were concluded at the end of Brezhnev's visit. Since early 1975, however, disquiet has on a number of occasions been voiced from Moscow concerning in particular the evolution of France's defence policy and its relations with the USA. When Russian press reports suggested that France's Atlantic policy was undergoing considerable modification (July 1975) Sauvagnargues felt obliged to deny the truth of the suggestions. Giscard's visit to Russia (October 1975) produced only modest results (some progress in technical and trade exchanges, slight shifts in the French positions on disarmament and European security) and created a somewhat negative impression: what were the Russians to think when while Giscard maintained his apparent goodwill towards them he also appeared more conciliatory towards the USA than either De Gaulle or Pompidou and (if the French communists were to be believed) was working towards a reintegration of France into the American-controlled defence systems of the West? That Giscard allowed senior ministers (in particular

Chirac and Interior Minister Poniatowski) to make lively anti-Soviet remarks in public did not help matters. In 1976 this state of ambiguity intensified: Russian reservations regarding the evolution of French military strategy became especially evident following the appearance of General Méry's article and, in spite of a bilateral agreement on nuclear accidents (July 1976), commentators stressed the growth of suspicion on the Russian side. In the early days of the Barre government, the new Foreign Minister, De Guiringaud, assured the Russian ambassador in Paris of the permanency of France's commitment to Franco-Soviet relations (September 1976). His predecessor Sauvagnargues had expressed similar sentiments over more than two years and it seemed that such formal efforts to dissipate Russian doubts would probably remain ineffective as long as they were divorced from apparent changes in French defensive strategy.

As Pompidou had done in 1969, Giscard set out in 1974 with a high determination to relaunch Europe. Even more than his predecessor Giscard had to pit his ideals against a Europe that was retrogressive and gravely disunited. Its problems were numerous: common monetary and energy policies were still lacking at a time when all member countries were experiencing more or less acute economic difficulties; American hostility to European initiatives was still in vigorous operation while, under Wilson, Britain sought to renegotiate its terms of membership and threatened to withdraw if its claims were not met; in the Autumn of 1974 farmers throughout the Community protested against inadequate agricultural prices. Little daunted, Giscard asserted (in May 1974) his hopes for a confederal union of Europe by 1980, independent of the USA with which periodic consultations and freely undertaken cooperation would nevertheless be desirable; fuller, franker exchanges with West Germany would be developed (whereas Pompidou had tended to look to the British link to counteract German influence within the Community) while the possibility of Franco-British coordination in the nuclear field would have to be explored, once a European defence system had been organized.

In a press-conference of October 1974 Giscard proposed a broadly two-fold method by which his ambitious dreams might be realized: Europe was to be built up again by both piecemeal, concrete changes (in other words, economic reforms) and by institutional developments (or, political construction). Neither has proved easy or particularly successful. Consistent with his electoral emphasis on the need for *concertation* rather than *confrontation* in international affairs Giscard refused French participation in the 'Group of 12' oil-importing countries: a common European energy policy appeared as far away as ever. The new, much vaunted cordiality between France and West Germany counted for little in fierce negotiations over the revision of agricultural prices (late 1974-early 1975) in the course of which Britain joined with Germany in pressing for a fundamental review of EEC agricultural policy. The modest results of the European summit held at Giscard's suggestion (Paris, December 1974) appeared to owe more to French concessions on the question of British contributions to the Community's budget than to a general reduction in the centrifugal tendencies of the nine partners. Things had not improved by the middle of 1976. Following an attempt (March 1976) to set up a steel cartel between Germany, Holland and Luxembourg (and therefore against the Coal and Steel Community) analyses of the impotent condition of the enlarged Community flourished; some observers even speculated sceptically on the future survival of the EEC's fundamental customs union.

It was clear that national interests had, in a time of international economic crisis, become too prominent and were working against European unity. Undeterred by such inauspicious circumstances French efforts to promote a politically united Europe have been persistent. Giscard's early tactics in this field owed much to the spirit of De Gaulle's European 'union of states': the new president suggested that the nine heads of government should meet together as informally as possible, three or four times a year, in order to discuss current or longer-term matters of European interest. Not surprisingly little by way of positive results emerged from the first of such meetings (held in Paris, September 1974) although much was made at the time of the improved ambiance among the European leaders. Included in Giscard's intentions in initiating this European Council was the idea of progressively accustoming the Nine to regular political discussion from which coordination and perhaps, almost by accretion as it

were, unity might emerge. Such a process would need to be
supported by significant institutional change, and here
cooperation was less readily forthcoming.

Although both Chirac and Sauvagnargues had pointedly
mentioned France's un-gaullist willingness to make certain
sacrifices of national sovereignty in the cause of European
integration (as though to prove its good faith France agreed to
abandon the use of the veto in minor discussions of the EEC)
the other partners largely failed to respond to Giscard's
enthusiasm (in late 1974) for a political summit. Since that
time however some progress has been made towards realizing a
major giscardian ambition, namely the creation of a European
parliament to be elected by universal suffrage. It was agreed in
Rome (December 1975) that the first election would be held in
1978 and a somewhat complicated allocation of national seats
in the future parliament (in line with a French proposal) was
decided in July 1976. While on the face of it the decision to
establish a democratically based European parliament must
appear an important advance, the prospects for this body from
the French point of view are unclear. The problem of the
impotence of the Community in many of its policy areas
remains as large as ever and does not encourage optimism
regarding the new institution's likely success. The first
European election, in 1978, will probably take place in the
same year as French legislative elections which appear likely to
produce a majority for the combined Left, a turn of events
which might well complicate matters relating to French
participation in a political Europe. Indeed criticism of
Giscard's pushing ahead with the Euro-parliament is not
lacking either from the Left or from among the gaullists of the
present majority: with varying nuances and in spite of
Sauvagnargues' assurances (August 1976) that the new
chamber would have no mandate to draw up a supranational
constitution, PCF, PS and UDR have all voiced their fears that
by such institutional means Giscard intends to establish an
'Atlanticized' Europe, aligned with and (the critics claim)
ultimately submissive to the USA. Following an official visit to
Britain and a further summit meeting with Schmidt (June and
July 1976) Giscard was thought to be trying to establish a *de
facto* triangular directorate within the Nine, based on Paris,
London and Bonn. Even assuming it survived, such an

arrangement appeared likely (especially to the PCF) to provide only a flimsy protection for French interests in any Americano-German Europe of the future.

For both economic and strategic reasons Giscard has developed relations with the Arab world to a point far beyond that reached by Pompidou. The French diplomatic position with regard to Israel shifted in emphasis if not in fundamentals when, in his press-conference of October 1974, Giscard stressed the vital importance of arriving at a durable settlement of the Palestinian problem, a settlement which had to include the establishment of sure and recognized frontiers for all concerned, and in particular for Israel and the Palestinian people. Coming soon after the French vote in the UN (14 October 1974) in favour of the participation of the Palestine Liberation Organization in a debate on the Palestinian question, Giscard's stand was not welcomed by Israel. With the mediatory role of the 1960s finished, French influence among the Arab countries has grown (at the expense of ties with Israel) for two main reasons. Firstly Giscard's moderation and insistence on negotiation in dealing with the energy crisis were appreciated by the oil-exporting Arab countries. Secondly, and more substantially, French economic involvement with the Arab world has expanded enormously in the last few years. Arms sales to the Middle East boomed after Giscard lifted the embargo (August 1974) while, conscious of the need to increase exports in order to pay for dearer oil imports, France has increased its industrial and technological sales to the Arabs as never before. In 1974 and 1975 the identification of French foreign policy with the promotion of trade missions was almost complete.

But not quite, since, as well as commercial interests, Giscard was concerned to pursue the wider Mediterranean policies initiated by Pompidou. To this end good relations were fostered with Greece (Giscard promised support in Greece's quarrel with Turkey over Cyprus, September 1975), Spain (France favours Spanish entry into the EEC and Juan Carlos was due to make an official visit to Paris, late in 1976), and the countries of North Africa. Following a successful visit to Algeria a few months previously, Giscard's prestige in the Arab world was boosted to new heights by the phenomenal popular acclaim he received in Morocco (May 1975). He used this and the platform afforded him by his visit to Tunisia (November 1975) to evoke the problem of the security of the Mediterranean, which he saw to be potentially menaced by the growing presence of forces of the two super-powers; in the future, he said, the region's security would have to be assured by the coordinated capacities of European, North African and Middle Eastern countries. Here Giscard goes beyond Pompidou's ideas for bilateral or even Franco-Mediterranean exchanges. It is generally accepted by all concerned that the concept of multi-form regional cooperation on the scale of the Mediterranean basin, free of interference from the super-powers, is one of immense potential but, with the EEC countries so often unable to agree among themselves on basic questions, such Euro-Arab dialogue has achieved only modest results. Moreover Franco-Arab relations have recently been subjected to set-backs. Early in 1976 Algeria was very critical of France on several counts: France had supported Morocco against Algeria over the Spanish Saharan issue, Giscard's alleged 'Atlanticism' was displeasing to socialist Algeria, as was the French president's reluctance to finance Algeria's development plans. The limits to French influence in the Middle East were made sharply apparent when (in May 1976) a modest, carefully conditional offer of French good offices in Lebanon met with a lively rebuff from a number of interested Arab nations. Based on an incorrect reading of the situation, Giscard's diplomatic intervention failed rather miserably.

France's relations with the Third World have recently been characterized by an instable combination — not unknown in De Gaulle's time — of generous intentions and imperfect realizations of those intentions. Since his election Giscard has consistently presented himself as a renovator of French cooperation policy. Long established links with North and Black African countries were to be retained, but also revised. In particular, the notion of imperialism was to be removed from cooperation in all its forms, technical, cultural or merely linguistic; *l'Afrique aux Africains* was the slogan Giscard used on several occasions in talks with African leaders in 1976. In consequence the numbers of French medical, teaching and administrative personnel based in Africa are diminishing gradually as France places more emphasis on cooperation through investment and the establishment of self-sufficient structures within the developing countries. Formation rather than assistance. More innovatory was the importance Giscard attached to the need to adopt international perspectives when considering the situation of the Third World. While France still had a useful role to play in Africa, in other areas limitedly national, bilateral action was insufficient: monetary, financial and commercial problems posed themselves on so large a scale that only a multi-lateral approach (involving effective negotiations between industrialized and developing nations) was appropriate. Appreciative reactions from parts of the Third World were provoked by Giscard's attempts to put his ideas into practice. In 1974 he insisted that all sides, and especially the oil-importing, non-industrialized countries, be represented at international energy talks. A conviction that a new, more equitable international economic order would need to be set up if an effective *rapprochement* between the developed and the developing worlds were to be possible lay behind Giscard's initiative in launching the Paris Conference on International Economic Cooperation (also known as the North-South conference). Other examples included a project for the nations of the West to establish an African aid fund by which major industrial and transport undertakings might be financed, and the suggestion (made in Zaire, August 1975) that copper importing and exporting countries should come together with a view to stabilizing the world copper market.

Many such enlightened proposals remained at the level of prestigious diplomatic initiatives, with little or no practical application. Even the North-South conference has yet to prove its worth: by July 1976 the Third World countries participating in it had become disillusioned and were complaining of the industrialized countries' reluctance to agree to reforms of the world's financial and commercial systems. Left-wing critics in France made much of the disparity between Giscard's loudly proclaimed internationalist views on cooperation and his equally evident determination to promote French commercial and industrial interests in Africa. Since 1975 moreover French prestige in Africa and among the nations of the Third World in general has declined. The complaints against France are varied, and on the increase: an ambiguous, pro-American role in Angola, interference in the Spanish Sahara, a vacillating conduct of policy over granting independence to the Comores and to the Territory of the Afars and Issas, the sale of two nuclear power stations to South Africa.... After the Organization for African Unity had expressed its discontent (August 1976) the summit conference of non-aligned nations (held at Colombo, also in August) condemned the nuclear sales to South Africa and called for an oil embargo against France.

De Gaulle's foreign policy appeared to be sharply defined and consistently pursued — for good or ill. Benevolent declarations have proved insufficient and the incoherence of Giscard's positions (in particular, on defence, relations with the USA and USSR, and with the Third World) is likely to draw more criticism from both inside and outside France.

Bibliography

Gaulle, C. De, *Mémoires de guerre*, 3 vols. Paris, Plon, 1954-9. Covers the period 1940-6.

———, *Mémoires d'espoir*, 2 vols. Paris, Plon, 1970 and 1971. Covers the period 1958 to early 1960s.

———, *Discours et messages*, 5 vols. Paris, Plon, 1970. The obvious primary source for the character, ideas and policies of De Gaulle. All these titles are also availabe in *Livre de Poche*.

Couve de Murville, M., *Une Politique étrangère 1958-1969*. Paris, Plon, 1971. An informative, but uncritical, account by De Gaulle's Foreign Minister.

Pickles, D., *The Government and Politics of France*, Vol. II: *Politics*. London, Methuen, 1973. Part II offers the fullest and most stimulating account in English available to date of foreign policy under De Gaulle and Pompidou (to late 1972).

Hartley, A., *Gaullism. The Rise and Fall of a Political Movement*. London, Routledge & Kegan Paul, 1972. Chapter Six on De Gaulle's foreign policy; a slighter alternative to Pickles.

Newhouse, J., *De Gaulle and the Anglo-Saxons*. London, André Deutsch, 1970.

Mendl, W., *Deterrence and Persuasion: French Nuclear Armament in the Context of National Policy, 1945-1969*. London, Faber & Faber, 1970. These two works are the most enlightening recent studies of their respective aspects of gaullist foreign policy.

Jobert, M., *Mémoires d'avenir*. Paris, Grasset, 1974. Jobert was a close associate of Pompidou before becoming his foreign minister. A lively, partisan account of foreign policy, covering in detail the period March 1973-May 1974. Also in *Livre de Poche*.

In both French and English, books on French foreign policy are numerous: the bibliography in Pickles (pp. 481-3) is most helpful. For an introduction to De Gaulle's foreign policy in the period 1958-69 see Keens-Soper, M., 'Foreign Policy' in *France Today*. London, Methuen, 1973 (second edition).

5 Education

Margaret Scotford Archer

An understanding of any element in the French system of education implies a knowledge of its history, precisely because a system existed in France a century before its development in England. The endurance of a structure designed to fit the needs of a pre-industrial society in the early nineteenth century leads to problems of adjustment to modern politics, economy and society. Even an understanding of the events of May 1968 requires that they should be seen not only as an attack on modern educational institutions but also on the traditional structure of the educational system as a whole.

The historical background

The dual tradition in French education. From the French Revolution onwards, two main traditions of educational thought and practice can be traced, whose conflict occupied the whole of the nineteenth century and has not been settled in the twentieth. On the one hand, the revolutionary emphasis on individual rights to instruction is most clearly expressed in the blueprints for educational reform put forward in the Assemblies of the First Republic. On the other, Napoleon's policy subordinated the amount and content of education received by individuals to the needs of state efficiency.

Condorcet's blueprint, the most influential on future educationists, summarizes the basic tenets of republican thought on education: instruction should be given because the individual has a right to it; it should therefore be universal and for both sexes, and ought to be common to all at primary level. By contrast, Napoleon's purpose in organizing a new educational system was pragmatic. Unlike the series of revolutionary blueprints which remained largely theoretical, his reforms were immediately implemented. Napoleon's two overriding aims of bringing about efficiency in the state and stability in society could not be served by treating unequals equally. Abandoning an educational philosophy based on individual rights for one which he framed in relation to state needs, he relegated primary education to the lowest priority in his policy. As the inculcation of useful skills was to be the supreme end of instruction, and as the state required only small numbers of trained individuals, any extension of training to the masses would be economically wasteful and socially dangerous. The minimal amount of knowledge the people required could be imparted in fee-paying or charitable schools, run by the Church. Therefore the state need not create primary establishments, but could content itself with controlling the loyalty of its teachers, who were mainly members of Catholic orders. Napoleon did not want the masses to be instructed beyond a minimum level of literacy, sufficient for the needs of a mainly agricultural economy, and did not object to their being religious, since the Church encouraged social conformity by preaching the acceptance of a pre-ordinated station in life.

Unlike primary schools, secondary and higher establishments were vital to the state, since they were to provide the skilled administrators, professionals and officers who were to serve it. As a corollary, state control over the education they gave and the degrees they granted would ensure that the best available talent would be channelled into useful occupations. In this way Napoleon justified the state monopoly over education embodied in the Imperial University of 1808 — the name given to the centralized system of state education. This prevented any other secondary school from functioning without direct authorization by the university authorities and submitted all state establishments to the control of a rigidly hierarchical administration, whose head was directly responsible to the Emperor. Not only did this centralization remain a permanent characteristic of French education, but many component institutions of the Imperial University have survived until now. Thus the *lycées* (state secondary schools), the *baccalauréat* (degree awarded for secondary studies and permitting university entry) and the *Ecole Normale* (training establishment for teachers who became civil servants upon admission to it) are still features of the contemporary system. Not only have such specific institutions endured, but the overall educational philosophy of the Imperial University is not yet extinct. Its fundamental principle, that if the state has no need of education, the people have no right to instruction, led to the development of a bifurcated system. On the one hand, highly specialized institutions at the secondary and higher level provided skilled servants of the state; on the other, limited instruction in primary schools sufficed to provide loyal citizens. The absence of a ladder between the two levels limited educational mobility and reflected the major social division between the bourgeoisie and the people.

The development of primary education under the July Monarchy. While Napoleon designed the educational system mainly to supply civil and military administrators, in connection with his policy of reconstruction in France and expansion abroad, subsequent regimes, without changing the basic structure of the Imperial University, modified some of its component parts. These reforms were largely dictated by the increasing pace of industrialization and the ensuing need for the propagation of some technical skills among the people. The July Monarchy (1830-48) was a predominantly bourgeois government, committed to industrial expansion and therefore disinclined to leave primary education to the Church, as under the Empire and the Restoration. The conservative bourgeois fear of elementary education as a source of social unrest — which had prevailed since the final phase of the Revolution — gradually gave way before the entrepreneurial awareness that industry required trained operatives. Hence the diffusion of primary schooling appeared a precondition of economic development and a prerèquisite of the July Monarchy's motto: *Enrichissez-vous.* However, the educational structure inherited from Napoleon was ill adapted both in its form and its content to the inculcation of the skills required. The main inadequacy was the gap between an exceedingly elementary primary schooling and an exceedingly classical secondary one. The nature of secondary and higher education made it irrelevant to industry, while that of primary schooling made it insufficient.

Thus the creation of *primaires supérieures* schools as an extension of primary schooling by the law of 1833 introduced the
degree of expansion in popular education, which the evolution
of the economy demanded and a stable society could accommodate. Considerations of economic utility rather than individual
rights to instruction prompted this reform. These higher grade
schools, created in 1833, and to which the best pupils passed
after completing primary studies, were predominantly vocational. They trained workers for commerce and industry,
without attempting to lead into secondary establishments.
Thus the basic bifurcation was unchanged. The educational
system had altered to meet economic needs, but had remained
socially conservative. The sons of manual workers could now
gain more instruction than previously without competing with
the children of the bourgeoisie, who still monopolized
secondary and higher education.

*The survival of the Napoleonic structure under the Third
Republic.* After the fall of the July Monarchy in 1848, the
Second Republic did not reform the educational system, but
reorganized the division of responsibilities between secular and
clerical teachers within the state system. This issue had
remained contentious since the Empire, as the Church sought
to retain its control over primary instruction and claimed a
greater share of secondary. The *Loi Falloux* of 1850 satisfied
these demands by reducing the educational qualifications
required from clerics and by giving the clergy seats on the
educational councils of the *Université*. Such concessions were
prompted by the fear of popular unrest, exemplified by the
excesses of June 1848, and by the reliance of the bourgeoisie on
religious instruction to restrain radicalism.

While the Second Empire (1852-70) was a period of religious
reassertion in education, the Third Republic gradually
secularized the state system and the separation of Church and
state in 1905 was the culminating point in this process. As a
result, the Church retained only 14 per cent of existing primary
schools (in 1906-7) and all its establishments, primary and
secondary alike, had to be fee-paying. Apart from the religious
issue, the main concern of educational policy under the Third
Republic was for numerical growth and institutional adapta-
tion within the Napoleonic framework.

Primary education. Throughout the century there had been evidence of a growing desire for instruction, witnessed by the spectacular development of adult education. The increase in school attendance predated the institution of compulsory and free primary education under the legislation introduced by Jules Ferry as Minister of Public Instruction in 1880. In a country that was still predominantly agrarian, this provision was particularly important for the rural areas, which had lagged behind the towns with regard to schooling. While it was gradually made universal, primary education remained detached from secondary but became more complex to meet the dual demands of increasing industrialization and growing parental aspirations. Thus it collected a series of additional courses, largely vocational in content, each regarded as terminal and leading to gainful employment rather than formal study. Simultaneously the higher grade schools broadened their curricula to include more modern subjects, in sharp contrast with the classicism of secondary establishments. While they, too, were terminal for most pupils, they came to supply some candidates for primary teacher training institutions. It is indicative of the isolation of primary instruction that its teachers should have been recruited from those who had no secondary education themselves. While additional courses and higher grade schools offered a modern and popular alternative to the classicism of the bourgeois *lycées*, the development of technical schools and centres of apprenticeship provided training facilities for future foremen, skilled workers and craftsmen. By 1919 it had become compulsory for primary school leavers to receive some form of vocational training until the age of 18. This growing differentiation within primary education mirrored the differentiation of the working class resulting from a more complex division of labour in industrial society. It did not, and was not intended to promote mobility from class to class, it merely diversified employment prospects for the working class.

Secondary education. Secondary curricula were intended to offer a preparation for higher education and the professions, and were therefore predominantly classical in content. Demands for the incorporation of modern subjects, the sciences and European languages, were in direct contradiction to the traditional structure of the *baccalauréat*. They met with considerable resistance from the supporters of a purely classical definition of culture. The adjunction of modern subjects was construed as a move away from the cultural role of education towards vocationalism. In this debate culture was seen as totally opposed to specialization: it was in fact defined residually as 'that which remains when all else has been forgotten'. This traditional approach was symbolized by the concentration on classical languages in the *baccalauréat* which was not modernized until 1902. From that date onwards, and as a result of parental pressures for a more practical curriculum, an alternative curriculum was introduced alongside the classical. Pupils could either opt for the classical or for the modern section, each of them leading up to a different *baccalauréat*. However, classicism retained its prestige and the best pupils were systematically channelled into the classical stream. Thus the direct connection established under Napoleon between classical studies and administrative or professional careers remained unbroken. The new modern stream reflected the growing demands of industry and commerce, which had grown in economic importance rather than in social prestige.

Higher education. Higher education within the Imperial University was designed to staff the two major professions of the time — the medical and the legal. The appropriate training was dispensed by Faculties of Medicine and of Law, which were self-contained establishments. On the other hand, the Faculties of Letters and of Sciences were mainly degree-granting bodies, which organized examinations, but did not have any permanent students. The main occupation of the professors was the organization and adjudication of the *baccalauréat*. Since future lawyers and physicians were trainees rather than students, the concept of student was unknown in France until 1877 and the few lectures given were addressed to the general public. The reform of 1877 was intended to turn the faculties into teaching bodies by increasing their staff and by creating state studentships. As a result, higher education experienced an enormous expansion, doubling its intake between 1875 (9963 students) and 1891 (19,281) and doubling yet again between 1891 and 1908

(39,890). However, this numerical increase tended to be concentrated in Paris (52 per cent of students in 1888). To offset this excessive centralization, which favoured Paris residents and was detrimental to provincial interests, a policy of founding regional universities was put forward in the 1880s. This aimed at the creation of true universities, teaching a wide range of subjects and grouping many students, rather than mere collections of isolated faculties. In other words, there was a protest against the Napoleonic structure with its rigid centralization and its narrow definition of higher education. The policy proposed was to extend the range of subjects in order to include the new sciences and to incorporate the neglected specialisms, such as archaeology or modern history. All disciplines were to be taught under the same roof. These pleas for reform failed, as the law of 1896 merely conferred the title of university upon groups of faculties existing in the same town, but did not amalgamate them into unitary bodies. Even if there were only two faculties in any one town, they were officially turned into a university, though neither their intake nor their courses changed. As a result, fifteen universities came into being, but their component faculties remained unaltered under this new name. Thus the law of 1896, generally considered as founding universities in France, actually destroyed the hopes of breaking away from the Napoleonic tradition.

The twentieth century

Plans for reform. Twentieth-century France inherited the Napoleonic educational system, virtually unchanged and characterized by the strict separation of primary and secondary schooling. This dichotomy firmly distinguished the bourgeoisie from the working class and the peasantry. As universal primary education threatened this distinction, the bourgeoisie strove to protect their privileged access to the *lycées* by sending their children to junior forms within the *lycée* (*classes élémentaires*), which were fee-paying when primary education had become free. The efficacy of this practice as a guarantee of admission to secondary education is illustrated by the numerical growth in the number of *lycée* junior pupils: from 16,000 boys in 1881 to 55,000 in 1940. Additional obstacles debarred working-class children from entry into secondary education — the length of the course that led up to the *baccalauréat* after seven years' study, the fees payable during this period were not completely covered by the grants available, the small number of these scholarships and their preference given to children of minor civil servants in the distribution (in 1911, 51 per cent of grants were awarded to children of civil servants and only 20 per cent to children of peasants, artisans and workers). The increase in popular demand for education was not met by an expansion of existing facilities at secondary level nor by a widening of recruitment. Therefore, it was the higher grade schools that absorbed the mass of pupils from primary school. This is evidenced by the fact that their intake in 1914 exceeded that of secondary establishments.

While in the nineteenth century it could be argued that the division into primary and secondary reflected the social structure of a predominantly agricultural country, the growth of the middle classes made this argument invalid in the twentieth. Nor could it be maintained that the adjustments whereby the primary system had developed its upper forms and the secondary its lower forms had made education more democratic. They had merely resulted in heightening class distinctions by inculcating two different cultures — excessive classicism among secondary pupils and extreme vocationalism among primary pupils. It is on these grounds that a reform movement advocating the integration of primary and secondary into an *école unique* was formed at the end of the First World War. Throughout the period between the two wars the debate about this reform was interrupted and largely unsuccessful. Indeed, while secondary establishments became free in 1928, they retained their traditional curricula and their social bias.

The main blueprint for *école unique* was produced by Jean Zay as Minister of Education in 1937. With its stress on equalizing educational opportunities and its acceptance of a universal right to secondary education, it is reminiscent of the revolutionary philosophy and stands in sharp distinction to the Napoleonic tradition. Zay advocated the creation of a middle school (*tronc commun*), which all pupils would attend between receiving primary instruction (common to all) and entry into secondary. The former courses of the *lycées* and of the higher grade schools would be integrated into a new secondary, divided into three branches of study: classical, modern and technical. The middle school would be concerned with guiding pupils to the appropriate stream of secondary studies according to their ability and interests. This proposal met with strong resistance, particularly from the unions of *lycée* teachers, and was only introduced in some establishments on an experimental basis. The war in 1939 and the collapse of the Third Republic prevented further debate on educational reform. After the interlude of the Vichy regime (which was strongly conservative in educational matters) the Fourth Republic was again faced with the issues that the Third had failed to solve. In 1947 the Langevin-Wallon plan, differing only in details from Zay's blueprint, was successfully resisted by the educationists' lobby. A similar fate was suffered by the Billères plan in 1957. Thus at the beginning of the Fifth Republic the dichotomy between primary and secondary remained almost intact.

The problem of democratization had not been solved; the main reason for this is instructive as it also accounts for failure to deal with the equally pressing issues of modernization and secularization during the same period. The answer lies in the fragmented nature of the political parties, and underlying this the cleavages dividing French society. In the first half of the twentieth century the political arithmetic of the multi-party system added up to Centre government — the alternation of power between Centre-Right and Centre-Left coalitions. Because of this political policy was reduced to the minimum programme which the governing coalition could agree to endorse, and legislation was restricted to the even more limited measures for which parliamentary support could be marshalled. This situation, commonly described as political *immobilisme* largely explains the long drawn out war of projects over *école unique*, which remained unresolved at the end of the Fourth Republic. In addition, however, the failure of the Left to hold together as a political force and to steer through the legislation sought by those it represented must also be held partly responsible.

The second aspect of the twentieth-century inheritance was the inability of educational institutions to satisfy demands for modern professional training, especially for the lower levels of industry, agriculture and commerce. 'Former le producteur, l'enseignement français y répugne. Son rationalisme tourne à l'intellectualisme'. This judgement of Prost's was particularly true in the field of technical and applied instruction at all levels. Certainly the Astier law of 1919 began to tackle the problem of producing a skilled workforce by founding part-time schools and making it obligatory for municipalities to run them, employers to release their apprentices, and working youths under 18 to attend. Its provisions initially implied decentralization, for such schools were to be controlled by the Ministry of Commerce, organized by local commissions, and financed by a tax on employers. However in the following years they were reintegrated with the Education Ministry and its successive directors steadily developed their general educational content at the expense of vocational specialization. As irrelevance increased so did evasion by apprentices and employers, such that by the outbreak of war apprenticeship training was still grossly deficient in quantitative and qualitative terms.

This tendency for specialized and practical training to be displaced by general education was even more marked at higher levels of technical instruction. There the creation of a series of national technical qualifications, each conferring rights to further education, resulted in uniformity rather than the diversity of skills required to match the occupational market. In particular the establishment of a *baccalauréat technique* in 1946 exerted a powerful downward influence, standardizing curricula in the upper reaches of the primary schools, the appropriate sections of secondary establishments, and the *écoles nationales professionelles*. In one way it might seem that this recognition signalled a break-through in modernization (for it meant a complete hierarchy of technical studies), but in the absence of decisive legislation establishing self-standing institutions free to develop their own approach, technical education was caught up in the traditional system and loss of specialization, diversity and practical relevance were the prices paid.

Thirdly the anti-clerical policy in education, pursued at the beginning of the century, by no means spelt a general consensus on the secular nature of public instruction.

Independent Catholic schools continued to attract a substantial number of pupils, although they were facing economic difficulties in their competition with the public sector. After the First World War this led protagonists of the confessional schools to launch a political campaign for governmental funding in proportion to their pupil intake. This particular formula was never successful, due to strong republican opposition, but after the introduction of free public secondary instruction the economic plight of the confessional schools progressively worsened and with it grew a determination to wrest support from the state in one form or another. Obviously this depended on a government favourably disposed to the Catholic educational cause, and it was not until the early fifties that the clerical issue could be politically reanimated. When, despite the vociferousness of its opponents, a law was passed in 1951 permitting state allocations towards teachers' salaries and buildings in the private sector, an MRP Deputy described this as the 'breach through which the flood will pass'. In other words the Catholic Parliamentary Association signalled its intention of achieving a much more far-reaching settlement than the politics of immobilism had allowed.

The Fifth Republic. While the powers of educational control remain concentrated at the Centre, this is the source of change, whether such transformations are initiated by political negotiation or induced by political disruption. Both processes were important under the Fifth Republic and their causes and consequences are closely intertwined. The first major reforms dealing with the problems of desecularization, democratization and modernization were directed by the government in a spirit of educational pragmatism. The situations it faced were inherited from the immobilism of the Fourth Republic and the dissatisfaction which had accumulated around these three issues. The Debré, Berthoin and Fouchet measures can all be looked upon in the same light, as piecemeal changes and pragmatic concessions intended to take the edge off discontent — giving away a little in order to conserve a great deal. As such these reforms tinkered *à la marge* rather than indicating a willingness to engage in large scale structural change or devolution of educational control. Public education remained, in the words of the then

Education Minister, Christian Fouchet, 'the biggest enterprise in the world apart from the Red Army' and was just about as responsive to the expression of social interests and local demands. In turn this rigidity was partly responsible for the outburst in May 1968.

Clericalism. The Debré law of 1959, giving state aid to private and mainly confessional schools, was justified by specific reference to the 'indispensable unity' of national education. This concession to Catholic supporters of government, which involved overriding the opinions of the vast majority of teachers' associations and trade unions, offered private schools one of four solutions to their financial difficulties — total integration with public education — a contract of association — a simpler contract — or the maintenance of the status quo. The first and last formulae were only used in a minority of cases, and by 1967-8 over 85 per cent of private primary and secondary schools were under one kind of contractual arrangement or the other. Both mean that the state aids such schools and pays teachers providing that, whilst conserving their 'own character', each school teaches 'with complete respect for liberty of conscience' and conforms to certain requirements about number of pupils, qualifications of teachers and standards of the physical environment. With the full contract all expenses are undertaken by the state at the cost of a serious loss of autonomy, for the school also becomes subject to the rules and programmes governing public education. The simple contract which provided for less aid, but less state control, was however only a temporary formula. Integration, loss of autonomy and standardization are all implicit in the Loi Debré. Its implementation leads one to wonder whether national education has not lost one of its few sources of diversity for it is difficult to see how such schools could preserve much of their 'own character' when forced to conform closely to public educational practices. De Gaulle had made the passing of this bill a matter of confidence (a sign that the new style of government was asserting itself in educational politics), and he secured his majority. What this Act did not do however, was to solve the clerical question in education. For the Church had lost in freedom what it had gained in funding, whilst defenders of *l'école laïque* were outraged at this manipulation of constitutional and govern-mental powers and organized massive demonstrations in favour of a single secular system of instruction. Significantly perhaps, these began in earnest in 1967, since a review of the Debré law was scheduled to start two years later.

Democratization. The Berthoin reform of 1959 came as an anti-climax after forty years of struggle to establish an *école unique*, and was intended to defuse and diffuse the discontent which had built up over the repeated failures of this movement. It was imposed imperatively by decree whilst De Gaulle still possessed the special powers granted to him before the new National Assembly had met. This compromise measure thus stemmed directly from the Presidency without there being opportunity for parliamentary intervention or modification.

A cycle of observation starting at the age of 11 and lasting for two years was introduced for all pupils. At the end of their elementary studies pupils could continue at primary school, attend a *collège d'enseignement général* (CEG was the new name for the old *cours complémentaires*), or enter a *lycée*. Officially this 'placement' (affected either by teachers' recommendations, parental preference, or simply by pupils staying where they were) was not viewed as decisive, for after two years of observation pupils would be oriented to the appropriate secondary course. In other words the observation cycle took place in different kinds of establishments, much to the satisfaction of the *professeurs* who had always opposed the idea of autonomous middle school for all. Moreover, the content of this cycle was not the same for all for it was made up of the normal programmes followed in the 6th and 5th class in these different kinds of institutions. The notion of a lengthy *tronc commun* followed by all pupils and used to establish the pattern of ability of individuals, was reduced to a single term during which syllabuses were 'harmonized' in different kinds of schools.

At the end of the cycle, the *conseil d'orientation* in each school advises parents on appropriate further studies. *Classes passerelles* situated in the 4th class provide conversion courses for those who had taken the wrong turning during the orientation phase. However since assessments are made in establishments varying from the *lycée* to the primary school, and moreover are made on the basis of their respective curricula, it is not surprising that this should result in very little individual mobility — only 1 per cent of pupils transferring from the latter to the former.

In respecting the vested interests of different groups of teachers, the compromise reform had left existing structures intact, but in doing so it had merely perpetuated these interests and the activities associated with their defence. Devices like the harmonization of curricula and the *classes passerelles* had certainly linked different parts of the system, but without providing the vast majority of pupils with more equality of educational opportunity. The dissatisfaction manifested by the primary and technical teachers, trade unions and political Left indicated that this decree was not the final solution to grievances which had rankled for half a century. Continued pressure from these quarters led the Minister to admit that the object of orientation was indeed defeated when it took place in different types of schools. Following this the *collège d'enseignement secondaire* (CES) was founded in 1963. Theoretically they were to cater for the whole age group from 11-14, thus functioning as common or comprehensive middle schools. Some pupils would proceed from the CES to secondary establishments, others to full time vocational training and yet others to apprenticeship schemes.

However, they were to be formed by converting the first cycle of *lycée* studies into independent units and by transforming existing CEGs, but this was opposed by *professeurs* and municipalities alike. Had the reform engaged in audacious structural change and created new polyvalent institutions of a self-standing type, it would have overriden vested interests: as it was it placed itself at their mercy. On the one hand conversion of schools was resisted (there were only 220 schools of this type in 1964 and 1,500 in 1968) with many still refusing to transform themselves in the seventies. On the other hand the CES was made up of a classical and a modern section from secondary, a *moderne court* section from the CET, and the old *classe de fin d'études* from the primary school, yet professional resistance has prevented fusion from taking place between them. The hope was that flexibility would replace separateness, to the benefit of all pupils, but this is not yet discernible outside a few pilot schools that have overridden the traditional curricula — inherited from the courses making up the CES. In sum the conversion modifying the Berthoin solution drew off little of the discontent stimulated by inequality of educational opportunity.

Modernization. The Fouchet reforms at secondary and higher level were a package of changes whose contents were intended to alleviate some very different kinds of discontent — that of students with the 50 per cent failure rate at the end of the first year (likened by a subsequent Minister of Education to organizing a shipwreck to find who could swim), of large employers with an encyclopaedic culture irrelevant to occupational needs, of staff at both levels with rising numbers and falling standards, and of the Left in general with its marked social discrimination. The same mechanism was adopted at secondary and higher levels and involved the differentiation of cycles of studies within them, giving a greater opportunity for vocational specialization. Simultaneously this was intended to satisfy students (by giving greater choice, better orientation and thus a lower failure rate), to produce school leavers and graduates better suited to occupational outlets, and to have a democratic appeal because it established shorter courses for those whose cultural or financial background had previously excluded them altogether. At university level the complementary reforms were mainly intended to obviate the disadvantages inherent in lack of pre-entry selection, for all holders of the *baccalauréat* had an automatic right of admission to higher education, without further test. Faculties of letters and science were reorganized by creating 3 cycles, the first one to provide the basic knowledge required to bring entrants up to university standard. This lasts two years and students choose a particular branch of study within each faculty, which leads to a diploma. Specialization becomes more intense in the second cycle, where after one year (i.e. 3 years of undergraduate study in all) the *licence* can be gained, or after two years (i.e. four in all), students can obtain the masters degree. The third cycle represents the beginning of post-graduate study.

In accordance with the philosophy of 'short' alternatives, a two year course for the training of *cadres* (at supervisory and lower managerial level) was given at new institutions, *instituts universitaires de technologie*, created alongside the university faculties. Staff were to be recruited partly from university teachers and partly from among specialists working in nationalized industries or private enterprises. The subjects taught were to be selected for their vocational value, assessed in the light of current economic needs, and teaching methods were to concentrate on practical projects in fields such as civil engineering, electronics, documentation and statistics.

These reforms were applied identically in all institutions, including the new universities created to cope with overcrowding. Even in broad technocratic terms they were less than successful, to judge from the divergence between the proportions intended to follow science and technology courses under the National Plan and the much lower percentage of students enrolling in them. Not only did this spell manpower deficiencies vis-à-vis the economy, but also the continued growth of a body of pupils and students without clear vocational expectations or opportunities. In addition, the chaotic application of the laws (more than 2000 decrees were involved) placed many students in an anomalous position because of these constant changes and heightened the awareness of many staff to continuous ministerial interference. Finally the Left was not impressed by the democratic intentions of a reform which created an inferior opportunity structure for the non-privileged by consistently directing them towards the 'shorter' alternatives, at all levels of instruction. Clearly many of the demands the reforms sought to assuage were mutually contradictory, but it is precisely because of this that any attempt to impose a uniform solution common to all schools and universities was bound to satisfy no one. Only a strategy which showed a willingness to sacrifice some control and allow some institutional autonomy, so that truly differentiated establishments could provide specialist services, could hope to satisfy conflicting demands simultaneously.

Groups inside and outside the system publicly registered their dissatisfaction with the educational policies of the Fifth Republic. The Caen Colloquium of university teachers meeting in 1966 rejected the Napoleonic concept of a single national structure, with identical regional establishments, as more suitable for the post office or police than for education.

Instead they sought the creation of diversified universities, autonomous in policy and administration, and for which the Ministry would merely ensure adequate financing, equipment and staffing. Such universities would develop their own courses, curriculum and examinations. The same demand for decentralization and the same condemnation of uniformity was issued in connection with secondary education at the Amiens Colloquium, only two months before the May events. But confronted with the highly controlled system there was little teachers could do at any level to introduce changes internally and thus to alter the nature of instruction from within. Given this position of powerlessness, the reactions of the teaching profession took two different forms.

Cut off from playing a constructive role in educational administration, or being able to respond directly to pupil requests or community requirements, much of the profession turned in upon itself and pursued an academic traditionalism which was not politically contentious. The cumulative effect of this reaction was to increase the gap between the nature of education and the facts of active life. In particular many teachers at secondary and higher level worked at reproducing themselves in their pupils and at reinforcing a *subject*-based organization of knowledge. For students the effect was to separate their present studies from any future relevance: for employers it was to deprive them of school leavers or graduates whose knowledge was organized on a *professional* basis. In his brilliant analysis, Pierre Bourdieu sums up the irrational situation which resulted as one where all were treated 'as apprentice professors and not as professional apprentices'.

At the same time, however, a different section of teachers turned to political action as a means of introducing change and pursued this end in conjunction with their professional associations, the trade unions and the left-wing parties. In 1967 the Communist Party published an issue of *l'Ecole et la Nation*, condemning Gaullist reforms as mere shunting operations, the *instituteurs'* syndicate passed a motion at its September Congress condemning government policy, and in November students went on strike at Nanterre over application of the Fouchet reforms. This signalled the growth of frustration shared by certain Parties, students and sections of the profession. However, it did not indicate the emergence of united action. Although teachers themselves had some unity within their professional federations, many teachers in turn were also members of the broader unions, the CGT and the CFDT, which were not themselves on good terms. Furthermore many university teachers and students looked to the parties and factions of the extreme Left which were viewed with the utmost suspicion by both the CGT and the Communist Party. Given that none of these groups, organizations or parties were in a strong enough political position to peacefully negotiate educational changes with the Gaullist majority government, the steady accumulation of grievances finally exploded into direct action — the May events. However, their internal divisions prevented them from forming other than temporary alliances, cemented by the euphoria of revolt, but never holding together for long enough to consolidate real educational gains.

The May events of 1968. The events taking place between May and June 1968 are frequently divided into three phases: the period up to 14 May, generally termed the university phase, saw the development of the student movement from Nanterre to the Sorbonne and to other universities, culminating in large scale street fighting and the famous 'night of the barricades'. The period between 15 and 27 May, frequently called the economic phase, witnessed the outbreak of strikes among technical and professional employees as well as industrial workers, reaching the unprecedented total of 8 million strikers, many of whom occupied their factories and workplaces. After this date followed the political phase of the crisis, in which the political parties and unions struggled to regain control of the situation and the defence of the Fifth Republic appeared less than certain. A vast amount has been written about the course of the events and the explanations advanced have been almost as numerous. These range from various kinds of conspiracy theory, through the official chain-reaction account (endorsed by Government and Communist Party alike) which interpreted the revolt as a fortuitous series of episodes tenuously linked by accident and opportunism, to explanations couched in terms of a new form of class conflict. There is not the space to review and assess such theories here, but only to make explicit that the present author tends to view the events as a whole as the explosion of a number of grievances which had accumulated over the decade as political closure replaced political immobility. More specifically, as an educational revolt, the events appear to have represented a massive condemnation of the mania for centralization and a movement for educational autonomy and regional diversity contrary to the revolutionary, monarchical and republican traditions alike. It now remains to be seen how far the reforms introduced in 1968 reflected a willingness to concede to these demands in order to solve the crisis.

The *Loi d'orientation de l'enseignement supérieur*, prepared by Edgar Faure, was a typical piece of panic legislation, adopted in the National Assembly by 441 votes to none, the Communists and 6 Gaullists abstaining. The major political parties had restricted themselves to textual criticism and minor amendments, the whole tenor of the debate being summed up by one Deputy who commended Faure's text for having the merit of existing. The parties of the Left no less than those of the Right had an interest in defusing the educational problem. In the face of virtual parliamentary unanimity on the bill, the teachers' associations and student groups were hopelessly divided — because the movement had never been fully organized, it had not been able to retreat, re-organize and reformulate its strategy after the electoral landslide. Thus no concerted extra-parliamentary opposition impeded either the passing or the implementation of the Act.

The *Loi d'orientation de l'enseigenement supérieur* was adopted by Parliament in November 1968 and broke away from the Napoleonic *Université* in each of the three main principles it endorsed — multi-disciplinarity, participation and autonomy. The speed of the operation was a condition of its success for these principles would never have received the almost unanimous support of Parliament had the scare been less recent. Indeed the grounds on which it was accepted or supported were very different — for some it was the fulfilment of long deferred hopes, for others it was an unavoidable concession intended to restore order. The law was construed by the Minister himself and by those who supported it on the Left as widening educational opportunities and increasing the share of students in decision-making processes. However the support of administrators and some of the Right was due largely to a desire for more emphasis on the vocational and their alliance with Faure proved temporary. Similarly the attacks made on the law before its enactment and which continued during its implementation sprang from a strange coalition between the conservative Right, the gauchist 'desperados' and traditionalist academics. This complex political background was important in shaping the interpretations given to the law in practice, especially as these often contravened both its spirit and letter. The vagueness of some provisions — due either to haste in drafting or the need for compromise — facilitated re-entrenchment.

The new law clearly embodied the concession of greater differentiation and specialization. The basic unit on which the whole system of higher education was to be founded was the university not the *Université*. Each university was to become an autonomous establishment from the financial point of view and free to draw up its own statutes — officially a complete departure from the previous centralized pattern, but like most of the provisions, one which was not to prove so radical in practice. Its size must be limited to avoid the huge conglomerations which had grown under the Fourth Republic, for the argument that large universities could offer a wider range of courses was considered less important than the advantage of specialization, preferably in accordance with regional characteristics.

Of the three characteristics with which the *loi d'orientation* endowed the new universities — multi-disciplinarity, participation and autonomy — the first attracted most attention and stimulated the keenest controversies among staff; the second pre-occupied the students virtually to the exclusion of all other issues. Yet it is autonomy which underpins them both and involves the greatest departure from previous practices. However as Maurice Duverger commented at the time the future of the universities was more dependent on the application of the law than its passing, and it is this which must now be examined.

Multi-disciplinarity. Limited in size *à l'échelle humaine*, the new universities are qualitatively defined as 'multi-disciplinary'. Article 6 of the law refers to the desirability of an interpenetration between arts-letters and science-technology as well as within them, whilst recognizing the possibility of 'universities with a dominant vocation', i.e. grouping related specializations. This was already tantamount to admitting that pluri-disciplinarity was a utopian ideal in the context of academic entrenchment in traditionally defined subject areas. The abolition of faculties — to which no mention was made in the first draft of the law, in order to kill them by omission, and to which only one article of the final text alluded — was to eradicate administrative and pedagogic barriers between disciplines.

Assemblies of staff — with or without the participation of students, depending on local conditions — were convened to decide on the reshaping of the former faculties and were free to do so without legal constraint. The only limitation on their planning was a maximum intake of 2500 students per unit, specified in the law. Thus a number of faculties survived under a new guise by constituting themselves into the new units for teaching and research. In larger towns, the pressure of student numbers forced a split into several units per faculty, but few original regroupings of subject matter within each unit were actually adopted. Almost everywhere, after less conventional proposals were put forward and then rejected by a majority, it was the solution most akin to traditional habits which was adopted, the sub-division by subjects. Thus faculties of science turned themselves into units of physics, chemistry, maths and natural science, whilst faculties of arts displayed an equal attachment to mono-disciplinarity. In other words a vertical division along the lines of the major courses taught in the past was the dominant pattern to emerge, rather than any radical reorganization of different knowledge systems in relation to one another.

Participation. By September 1969 some 630 units had been set up to replace the former faculties (approximately 100) and endowed with statutes. According to the *loi d'orientation* a complex procedure of elections was organized separately for each category of teachers, students, administrative and technical staff. If they failed to agree on the statutes by March 1969, these could be introduced by governmental decree. The complicated conditions with which the law surrounded representation of each category were intended to protect the interests of the professoriate without depriving other members of staff, and to grant an opportunity for participation to students. The established university teachers were given 60 per cent of staff representation although they only made up about one-third of the total teaching personnel. The parity between staff and students, promised in the aftermath of the May events, was in fact reduced to a maximum of one-third for students because of the distinction made between university teachers in terms of seniority. Furthermore the limits imposed on participation are broad and exclude such areas as the drawing up of teaching programmes, the allocation of credits, the testing of aptitude and knowledge, the recruitment and promotion of staff, and all matters of selection. In sum this legal hedging contrasted sharply with the initial statements about equal shares in university management.

Unwilling to participate in the reorganization of what they termed 'bourgeois universities', the *groupuscules* and the French Union of Students itself pronounced against their members voting in the first university elections. The main grounds on which they advocated abstaining were the advantages granted to the professoriate and the restrictions on student representation, together with the inclusion of local personalities in the Councils (between a sixth and a third of their membership), a symptom to them of the subordination of the university to the interests of large firms, under cover of participation. In fact this attitude may have been widespread as only one student in four votes on average in Council elections. However, whether as a result of political involvement or apathy, student representation turned out to be insufficiently representative, often improvised on the spur of the moment and generally inadequate in between elections.

The first responsibility of the Council elected within each unit was to meet the Councils of other units with which the creation of a university was contemplated. This cumbersome process was suggested by Minister Faure as implementing the spirit which had prevailed in May — a return to grass roots, the initiation of reforms from the basic cells in contrast to the centralized tradition of making decisions at the top and transmitting them downwards. The law itself remained unfortunately vague about the eventual administrative autonomy of the units in relation to the powers of the new universities. It was largely fears about the latter which prompted most units to play safe by avoiding any cooperation with others which were unfamiliar, competitive, or politically uncongenial. Thus 'compromising' entanglements were avoided, and in the process few experimental combinations emerged. Most pure scientists found the social scientists too politicized for comfort, as did lawyers, and the former association between letters and social sciences within the old letters faculties tended to endure in the new universities. The faculties of sciences and medicine, well endowed with research laboratories and staff, did not like to merge with poorer specialist areas for fear of having to share resources. The Ministry certainly opposed attempts to set up purely medical (or legal, or technical) universities in order to uphold the principle of multi-disciplinarity, but as a result partnerships were often based on shared political attitudes rather than intellectual complementarity, a 'marriage of reason' between law and medicine being a common pattern.

Autonomy. Prior to 1968 very little pedagogical autonomy prevailed as the faculties were not free to select their students (since the *baccalauréat* gave automatic right of registration), nor to devise their own curricula (which were drawn up by the Ministry), nor to issue their own qualifications. In other words the inputs, processes and outputs of higher education were not determined by academics themselves but were regulated by the Ministry. Furthermore the staff were centrally appointed under the civil service statutes and thus in no sense did the faculty make up a self-constituted or self-regulating body. The reform touched upon each of these aspects and its overall effect was a formal increase in academic freedom. That its impact has been less marked in practice is due to various factors, among which the conservatism and vested interests of large parts of the academic body should not be under-estimated. On the other hand it is understandable that the experimental excesses taking place in one or two institutions, which exploited their formal rights to the limits, were counter-productive in convincing many that the only defence of academic standards lay in clinging to the traditional framework of teaching and learning.

In the past the major limitation on academic freedom derived from the existence of national degrees and diplomas which meant that the corresponding courses would be based on ministerial regulations. The new universities are now free to issue their own certificates, but even the most extreme opponents of centralization have been unwilling to relinquish the state guaranteed qualifications which future employers still seek. However the scope for experimenting with curricula and even teaching methods remains restricted since all units and universities are constrained to recognize each other's programmes. To these pressures in favour of homogeneity is added the right of students to be offered a similar bill of fare since they are not free to choose their own cafeteria — the university in which they register must be the closest to their domicile. This limitation, intended chiefly to prevent the exodus of provincials to Paris, makes it impossible, at least in the first cycle to select from among various curricula and approaches. Hence the alternative was either the arbitrariness of geographical origin or uniformity between universities at the level of the first cycle. Historical precedent has influenced most academics in the latter direction, and experiments with new specialist subjects and approaches have largely been confined to the second and third cycles and to certain isolated institutions.

The seventies and the aftermath. For those who had sought educational change through direct action, the May events were disintegrative in two different respects. On the one hand the failure to impose the transformation desired caused the membership of many participant organizations to sink. This was particularly true of the UNEF (Students' Union) which collapsed into a number of factions, the largest being the communist dominated *UNEF-Renouveau*. In turn this meant that just as the legal influence of students in university administration was recognized, their disorganization and factionalism made them completely ineffectual. On the other hand the links which had temporarily been forged between different kinds of educational interest groups were broken, and with them the opportunity for aggregating educational grievances was lost. The breach between the two main trade unions widened with the CGT reaffirming *its* concern with concrete wage settlements and condemning the leftist trend in the CFDT as 'revolutionary infantilism'. Simultaneously however, both closed union ranks, shrinking from the destructive influence of extreme Left parties and groups, and stressing their traditional independence from all political parties. This attitude was also marked in the *UNEF-Renouveau* which restored primacy to educational issues. But this rejection was reciprocal, the official political parties being equally wary of student activism and the Communist Party being as cautious as others in this respect.

The early seventies were thus a period of enduring grievances and continuing disunity. The 1968 law seeking to modernize the university provided little satisfaction for the student body. Their political factions, banned after the events, reformed themselves with increased optimism about a 'proletarian alliance' and an overt commitment to violent action. Yet this resurgence of faith in the revolutionary character of the working class has been accompanied by few signs of its willingness to provide carrier organizations, in part only because of stricter union surveillance. This has resulted in the common pattern of violence being turned inwards against the university itself. The outbreaks taking place in 1970 showed very little attempt being made to find an educational nail upon which to hang a political confrontation. Nevertheless these are the groups, together with their sympathizers among the teaching staff, who may be expected to react violently against any further modernization which harnesses higher education more closely to the mixed economy. On the other hand the majority of students who, without enthusiasm, seemed prepared to wait and see the outcome of the reforms retain realistic grievances about the divorce between university and active life.

It is not only the modernization issue which has left behind it seething discontent. An amendment to the Debré law in 1970 brought the old anti-clerical pressures to the surface and indicated that official policy towards Catholic schools hinges on the continuation of a rightist majority. Similarly the virulence of debates about the teaching of Latin, a smoke-screen behind which the battle for equality of opportunity is fought out, shows the question of democratization to be unresolved. Given disunity among the discontented parties, their grievances are likely to grow for they will not be able to exert effective political pressure. The pattern of accumulation of dissatisfaction and its ultimate explosion into direct action seems likely to continue, but the next outburst is itself conditional upon this very disunity being surmounted.

Bibliography

The books recommended below refer to the two parts of this chapter.

The historical background

Anderson, R.D., *Education in France 1848-1870*. Oxford, Clarendon Press, 1975. A detailed historical account with an extensive bibliography.

Barnard, H.C., *Education and the French Revolution*. Cambridge University Press, 1969. Contains almost the only detailed account in English of the ideas and legislation of the Revolutionary assemblies and their notion of education as a natural right for all.

Prost, A., *L'enseignement en France: 1800-1967*. Paris, Colin, 1968. Perhaps the best account existing to date on the historical changes in the French educational system; contains extracts from major reform bills and influential authors.

Vaughan, M. and Archer, M., *Social Conflict and Educational Change in England and France. 1789-1848*. Cambridge University Press, 1971. A comparative sociological approach to educational development in the two countries.

The twentieth century

Archer, M.S. (ed.), *Students, University and Society*. London, Heinemann, 1972. Chapter 6 presents an analysis of the May events.

Bourdieu, P. and Passeron, J-C., *Les Héritiers, les étudiants et la culture*. Paris, Minuit, 1964. An extremely good summary of the influences of pupils' social origins on school and university entry, followed by an analysis of the contemporary student condition.

Fournier, J., *Politique de l'Education*. Paris, Seuil, 1971. An excellent review of contemporary educational problems and their relationship to the political structure.

Fraser, W.R., *Reform and Restraint in French Education*. London, Routledge & Kegan Paul, 1971. An examination of the difficulties of introducing educational change in a highly centralized system.

Talbott, J.E., *The Politics of Educational Reform in France 1918-40*. Princeton University Press, 1969. The best account available in English of the *école unique* movement before the second world war.

Touraine, A., *Le Mouvement de Mai ou le Communisme Utopique*. Paris, Seuil, 1968. Provides a very controversial interpretation of student unrest in terms of the changed position of students in the class structure of technological society.

6 The Church

J. E. Flower

Introduction

In January 1976 the *Mission de France* issued the following statement: 'Dix ans après Vatican II, la perspective ouverte au concile nous apparaît toujours aussi urgente: mettre fin aux croisades idéologiques, aux condamnations et aux interdits, pour entrer dans le temps du dialogue et du service.' To many, such words must have seemed to be just one more jaded statement of the obvious. If any one issue can be said to have dominated the history and development of the Catholic Church and its policies in France during the first three quarters of the twentieth century, it is precisely the need for it to become accessible to the vast body of people and thereby relevant to their normal lives. Nor indeed would it be true to say that it alone has been preoccupied by this need. The *Fédération Protestante de France* (which represents approximately 800 thousand people) has regularly debated it at its triennial congress, and in 1972 published its fullest statement to date in *Eglise et Pouvoirs*. Whether or not any statistically measurable progress has been made, however, is not easy to judge. In terms of the actual structure and organization of the Catholic Church erosion appears to be widespread: there has been a steady decrease in the numbers both of seminarists (1790 in 1973-4; 1509 in 1974-5) and of ordinations (489 in 1967; 219 in 1973; 170 in 1974); a growing number of parishes are without priests; membership of religious orders is falling quickly; too many bishops (average age 61) are at or beyond the age of retirement; attendance at Sunday mass has reduced since 1971 by 40 per cent. Yet over 90 per cent of the population is still baptized into Roman Catholicism, the faithful continue to stream to Lourdes in their many thousands, and if reading habits can be taken as evidence of the relevance of religion to modern living the circulation numbers of the daily *La Croix* (140 thousand) and weekly *Témoignage Chretien* (50 thousand) are impressive. The most significant indications of how religion still remains a vital ingredient in the life of the French nation, however, have been on the one hand the increase in left-wing Catholic groups (*Echanges et Dialogue, Chrétiens marxistes révolutionnaires, Chrétiens pour le socialisme*, for example) — so marked in fact that it prompted the PCF leader Georges Marchais to appeal in June 1976 to Catholics and Communists to join forces — and on the other, a sudden resurgence of traditionalism which came to a head in the same year around the controversial figure of Marcel Lefebvre.

Catholic Action: the early years

Modern Catholic action in France has its roots in the efforts of a number of prominent lay Catholics like Albert de Mun, René de la Tour du Pin, Léon Harmel and above all Marc Sangnier who, during the last years of the nineteenth century, attempted to give practical expression to Pope Leo XIII's policy of *ralliement*. This policy, continued after the First World War by Pius XI who referred to Leo XIII as his 'spiritual father', was essentially an attempt to encourage French Catholics to accept the republican government and to make the Catholic Church an accessible and meaningful institution for the working class. Once traditional barriers and attitudes had been broken down spiritual unity and national solidarity would develop to mutual advantage. The task was a difficult one however. Whatever political and social changes may have occurred since the late nineteenth century, the view that the Church should represent authority and discipline died hard. Maurras, whose right-wing extra-parliamentary movement, the *Action Française*, campaigned for a restoration of the monarchy and propounded a political philosophy based on the principles of heredity and social hierarchy, had not only found a perfect proto-type in the structure of the Catholic Church but also a ready ally during the immediate

pre-war years in Leo's successor Pius X. Remembered today
for his strict conservatism (his policy centralizing the Church
firmly on the Vatican became known as 'integrism') Pius
attacked all attempts at compromise with democratic republican ideas or systems. With hindsight it is tempting, of course,
to see his policies as an obstacle to a course of events which had
already become apparent. At the time, however, Pius was in a
difficult position. The growing anti-clericalism of the Third
Republic had come to a head in 1904-5 when Emile Combes
had broken off diplomatic relations with the Vatican. Perhaps
Pius X was repaying the minister's intransigence in kind, but
his attitude did sound a warning note for all subsequent
attempts to draw Catholicism and matters of political and
social importance too close together.

In the early twenties and in a political climate in which the
Left was becoming increasingly influential and in a spiritual
one generally referred to as a state of dechristianization, Pius
X's rigid policies were replaced by Pius XI's attempt to
introduce a second *ralliement*. With the disastrous reduction
in the number of priests — a direct consequence of war
casualties — Pius saw that there was now more than ever a
need for lay participation in ecclesiastical matters. In 1929, for
example, he remarked: 'Le clergé actuel ne suffit malheur-
eusement plus aux besoins de notre temps ... Aussi est-il
nécessaire que tous se fassent apôtres; que le laïcat ne se
prenne pas dans une indifférence boudeuse, mais prenne sa
part dans la lutte sacrée...'. It was clear, however, that for the
young in particular the institution of study circles of the type
that had been encouraged during the last twenty-five years or
so of the nineteenth century was too intellectual a method:
instruction, it was thought, should be replaced by example.
Youth groups within different social environments were
established, all of them affiliated to the *Association Catholique de la Jeunesse Française* (ACJF) — itself founded long
before in 1886 — but retaining their own distinctive autonomy. Of these the *Jeunesse Ouvrière Chrétienne* (JOC) was
the first (1926), soon followed by a number of others: *Jeunesse
Agricole Chrétienne* (1929), *Jeunesse Etudiante Chrétienne*
(1930), *Jeunesse Maritime Chrétienne* (1932), *Jeunesse Indé-
pendante Chrétienne* (1936). The problems involved varied
from group to group; the JAC, for example, which drew its

membership from a society that already accepted the traditions of the family and the village as its base, was less spectacular in its early achievements than the JOC whose members were at best apathetic towards religion and who regarded the church as a stronghold of the bourgeoisie. Similarly the JEC tended to become occupied with a number of ideological and sentimental considerations, which undermined the stability of the faith that it was hoped would predominate.

Whatever their developments, however, no one of these groups allowed itself to move beyond the limits set upon its activities by the central ecclesiastical body in France, the *Assemblée des Cardinaux et des Archevêques* (ACA), which had been established in 1919. Yet while even the JOC was able for the most part to comply with Pius's wishes and remain apart from party politics, it was inevitable that with such a deep concern for the working class one of the most striking features of this period should be the relationship between Catholics and communists. At this time essential ideological differences made any deep *rapprochement* seem impossible, and in spite of a number of statements in the *Osservatore Romano* (the *Pravda* of the Vatican as it has been described) encouraging tolerance, many Catholics remained openly hostile. As General Castelnau, leader of the conservative *Fédération Nationale des Catholiques* maintained, communists were atheists, subversive elements in society, and quite beyond salvation. The matter was complicated even more by the growing threat of fascism. The Italian invasion of Ethiopia and the Spanish Civil War both provoked extremist reactions. Over the latter in particular French Catholics almost as a whole at first accepted the simplist formula of the Church versus heathens, and talked in terms of a crusade. Gradually, however, more and more of them sympathized with the republican position and deplored Rome's reluctance to condemn the extreme Spanish Right. Such approval for the side to which communists also gave their support added a further dimension to a situation that had already arisen internally in France in matters of industrial dispute. The 1936 elections revealed that the communists, whose numbers had increased tenfold during the last few years, were by now a real political force. On 17 April their leader Maurice Thorez made his famous appeal for collaboration: 'Nous te tendons la main, catholique, ouvrier, employé, artisan, paysan, nous qui sommes des laïques, parce que tu es notre frère, et que tu es comme nous accablé par les mêmes soucis.' When in the following year Léon Blum echoed Thorez and suggested that collaboration was not only possible but desirable, *Sept*, the Catholic weekly, printed his words. In September the paper was ordered by Rome to cease publication; such an open declaration of sympathy was not to be tolerated, and for all his progressive measures Pius XI, like his predecessors, was adamant that religion should be above and quite distinct from the affairs of the political world.

Catholics and the Occupation

In his *Histoire de Catholicisme en France* André Latreille suggests that the Second World War stifled the promise of the 1930s, and in terms of a continuous development of the various groups that had been formed during these years this is largely true. But after a period of uncertainty the experience of war and the Occupation led to a number of developments that were to have far greater significance than anything previously undertaken, and of these the worker-priest experiment is the best example.

Under the catalytic influence of the Occupation the French people's sense of religion was expressed as it had been after 1870-1 in highly emotive terms. Divine punishment was the inevitable and just result for the sins of the Third Republic — a theme taken up by Camus in *La Peste*. As general Weygand remarked: 'La France a mérité sa défaite, elle a été battue parce que ses gouvernements depuis un siècle ont chassé Dieu de'lécole.' However aware the Church may have been of the dangers of the Occupation, it was hardly in a position of authority, and some of its high-ranking members, more politically astute than others perhaps, saw that they should make the best of the situation. Cardinal Gerlier, Bishop of Lyons, advised Catholics to group themselves around Pétain who was greeted in 1940 by Gerlier himself as a kind of providential hero: 'La France avait besoin d'un chef qui la conduise vers son éternel destin. Dieu a permis que vous fussiez là.'

None the less, there were at the same time other leading

ecclesiastics who were aware of the dangers inherent in such idolatry. Feltin, Archbishop of Paris, remarked in 1941 that respect and deification should not be confused: 'le respect dû à l'autorité ne demande pas que nous déïfions celui qui la personnifie'. Yet in general Gerlier's views were predominant and in 1941 the French episcopate published a declaration of loyalty to the Pétain regime, even though it cautiously suggested at the same time that actual political commitment should be avoided. During the following months more statements on these lines from important members of the French Church were pumped out by the *Services d'information de Vichy* with, if necessary, censorship of the more cautionary passages. It was not long before the effect of such propaganda could be seen, partly in the form of a Pétain cult accompanied by invocations, poems and prayers (including a parody of the Lord's Prayer), and partly in an appeal for a renewal of the militant Christianity of the Middle Ages, a theme which had been popular during the last years of the previous century and which is also central to the political ideas of Catholic writers and intellectuals like Bernanos and Maritain. Moreover, the Vichy slogan of *travail, famille, patrie* was also likely to appeal to those many Catholics who saw the growing readiness to agree to a liberal interpretation of their faith and the flirtation with communism as real threats to the stability and traditions of Catholicism.

Yet this, as Jacques Duquesne has remarked in his book *Les Catholiques français sous l'occupation*, is a rather one-sided and even unfair picture. There were from the very beginning of the Occupation signs of resistance among Catholics, voiced in particular by *Le Temps présent*, a left-wing Catholic paper, which had been founded as a successor to *Sept* by, among others, Jacques Martain and François Mauriac. But large-scale participation by Catholics in the Resistance movement was comparatively slow in developing. The dissolution of the trade unions, the CFTC and the CGT in 1940 (an action which, ironically perhaps, drew their leaders closer together), the growing drain on French manpower for the *Service du travail obligatoire* (STO), and the large-scale deportation of Jews in 1942, however, were sufficient reasons for inducing action. On the second of these issues Rome remained silent and it was left to Cardinal Liénart to take the initiative. He argued that Catholics as a whole and regular clerics in particular should accept this as a challenge and should feel responsible for those in Germany whom they were to join, whatever their political or religious beliefs. At the same time in France itself the appeal of the central church authority, the *Assemblée des Cardinaux et des archevêques*, to respect the legitimacy of the Vichy regime was swept aside by a wave of indignation hardened by an awareness of the increasing viciousness of reprisals against civilians and by the arrests of some higher members of the clergy. It was such realizations as these that began to draw Catholics and left-wing Resistance fighters together; here was the opportunity that had been sought already on several occasions in the past.

In the early 1940s a number of positive steps were taken, which were to lead to important post-war developments in the sphere of Catholic Action. In 1941 the *Mission de France* was founded by Cardinal Suhard in an attempt to train priests to form part of an inter-diocesan body that would reach out into the dechristianized areas of France. Two years later a book written by two Paris chaplains, the abbés Daniel and Godin, *France, pays de mission*, argued that the continuing association of Catholicism and the bourgeoisie not only rendered the former unknown to the workers but, more importantly, *unknowable*. This view, together with the situation in Germany, had much to do with the creation in the same year (1943) of the *Mission de Paris* from which the worker-priest experiment essentially sprang. We should remember, however, that at its inception the worker-priest experiment was not a large-scale undertaking, and that similar ideas were developing at the same time and in different ways.

Post-war developments

After the war Pius XII emphasized once more the eternal and absolute qualities of the Church, but at the same time made it clear that its immediate task of missionary work was vital. While participation of lay Catholics in this was to be encouraged, some of the Pope's statements indicated that control by senior ecclesiastics was imperative if a second *ralliement* was to be avoided. In spite of such encouragement, however, it should not be imagined that there was a great resurgence of religious fervour. After the war the pattern of dechristianization that had characterized the 1920s was still as apparent, and the recovery in the numbers of the clergy that had been achieved by the late 1930s had been lost. But many of the lay Catholics who were active were so in a new way. They were less inclined to consider politics as a danger to their spiritual state and also their Resistance record meant that they were more readily accepted. Indeed the first ministry of the provisional government contained five former members of the general committee of the ACJF and the MRP in its early years at least enjoyed the support of a number of bishops.

Since the war, the more regular developments of Catholic Action can, in a general way, be divided into three different categories: Catholic Action groups continuing the work of those established in the 1930s, the whole of the worker-priest experiment, and various attempts to reform certain aspects of the ecclesiastical structure and its traditions.

Catholic Action groups. These were plentiful in number and far more varied in outlook than their predecessors some twenty years before. Some, like the *Action Catholique Ouvrière* (ACO) formed in 1950, remained relatively conservative in their aims and, while the ACO was concerned, as its name suggests, with working-class areas of France, it managed on the whole to remain apart from political commitment. Others were not so cautious. The *Ligue Ouvrière Catholique* (LOC), for example, founded during the war as a body to be responsible for providing aid for prisoners and refugees, turned, in later years, towards politics with the ultimate result that it was disowned by the ACA in 1945, and in the following year changed its name to the *Mouvement de Libération du Peuple* (MLP). One further group worth noticing is the *Jeunesse d'Eglise*. This already existed before the war and is important for the impetus and encouragement it received from the abbé Montuclard whose critical attitude towards the church's organization and policy caused the Vatican some concern. Religion, he argued, was badly presented in the world. His support for the working class was in many cases extreme: 'la classe ouvrière redeviendra chrétienne, mais ce ne sera pas vraisemblablement qu'après qu'elle aura elle-même par ses propres moyens, guidée par la philosophie immanente

qu'elle porte en elle, conquis l'humanité.' Such outspoken-
ness as this, published in particular in his book *Les
Evénements de la foi*, was so disturbing that it was put on the
Index in 1953.

Less extreme in its various pronouncements (though no less
ambitious in its aims) was the *Mission de France*. Founded in
1941 as an inter-diocesan association by the ACA, it provided
a special training for the priests it sent to work in teams in dechristianized areas. In this, as we shall see, it differed
significantly from the worker-priests who worked individually
and who were criticized by the *Mission de France* for doing so.
At first the *Mission* directed its attentions to rural areas, but
gradually realized that it was in the towns that its activities
were most needed. Soon, however, its priests were to be
criticized by the bishops with whom they were meant to work
in close collaboration. In 1952 and 1953 they complained (like
the worker-priests) that the Vatican had very little idea of what
was happening in the dechristianized areas of France. Also in
1953 rumours of Marxist literature being read by the
seminarists prompted an investigation and in August the
Mission was closed to await a new statute to be promulgated by
Rome. In the following year the new conditions of the
Mission's activities were published, and it was now noticeable
that only those bishops who actually requested the assistance of
priests from the *Mission* had them; moreover, an episcopal
Commission was set up to be responsible for them and to give
them their directives. However disappointing such centralization and control may have appeared to some members of the
Mission, an attempt had been made to create an organic unit
within France which would link missionary priests, Catholic
Action groups and the general clergy. In so doing, the *Mission
de France* looked forward to the later phases of the worker-
priest experiment: the idea of a mission for the dechristianized
working-class areas was being kept very much alive.

Worker-priests. When the Vatican finally decided to discon-
tinue the first phase of the worker-priest experiment in 1954,
Cardinal Feltin, Archbishop of Paris, summed up the views of
many who were sympathetic to the movement with the
following words: 'Le monde ouvrier, éloigné de l'Eglise, a son
histoire, ses traditions, ses valeurs morales, ses richesses

spirituelles et une certaine unité qui fait qu'il n'accepte pas l'étranger à son milieu qui vient lui donner des leçons. Pour exercer sur lui une influence, il faut être naturalisé, reconnu comme membre de ce monde.'

Attempts to take Catholicism to the working-class world had, as we have seen, been various, but none had sought to penetrate it in such a total way as the worker-priest experiment. Individual priests had already made some efforts before the war: the Franciscan Bousquet or the Dominican Loew, who went respectively to Ivry and Marseilles, were well in advance of the general movement created during the years of the Occupation. In many ways those priests who went to Germany found themselves in an artificial situation, and their complete independence was not something from which worker-priests in France were subsequently to benefit. In *France, pays de mission*, Daniel and Godin outlined some of the major problems to be faced: the working-class conception of the Church as a capitalist stronghold must be overcome, the priest should assimilate himself completely with his new environment and only when accepted reveal his true identity, and also there should be some kind of preparatory training. While these points were recognized they tended to be over-ambitious. Assimilation quickly led in many cases to complete identification, with political and emotional ties becoming particularly strong. As one worker-priest remarked: 'Le fait formidable, c'est que lorsqu'on devient ouvrier, le monde bascule du côté ouvrier.' Although a number of them disagreed with Gilbert Cesbron's portrayal of the worker-priest's dilemma in his novel *Les Saints vont en enfer*, the fact remains that they were very much alone, regarded often with suspicion by more traditionally minded Catholics and by their bishops, who had little or no conception of working-class conditions. Such a situation could lead only to friction and discontent, and in 1951 uneasiness in Rome led to a suspension in recruitment. In 1952 two worker-priests were arrested in a communist-inspired demonstration against General Ridgway when he arrived as Allied Commander in Europe, and in the following year the experiment was stopped altogether and the priests withdrawn. The majority of them obeyed Rome's decision without hesitation, and in January 1954 a number were linked with the teams trained by the *Mission de France* and known as 'prêtres de la mission ouvrière'. For some worker-priests, however, the Vatican's decision was little more than a betrayal, while, more embarrassingly still, the three French cardinals at that time (Feltin, Suhard and Gerlier) all approved of the experiment and yet were bound to enforce the ban. Outside the Church, militant lay Catholics, particularly those in the JOC and the ACO, were quick to criticize: 'L'Eglise nous a trompés deux fois, une première fois en ne s'occupant pas de nous malgré ses promesses, une seconde fois en s'occupant de nous par les prêtres-ouvriers pour nous les retirer quand ils n'ont plus fait ce qu'elle voulait.'

Such criticism as this, together with considerable sympathy and pressure within the Church itself, was sufficient to ensure that the ban could only be short lived, and in 1959 Cardinal Feltin made a specific request to Pope John XXIII for it to be lifted. John refused, principally on the grounds that there was no reason why the ultimate result should not once again be one of incompatibility, a view that was not all that surprising perhaps when we learn that it was John, as papal nuncio in Paris, who had sent unfavourable reports of the worker-priests' activities to Rome several years before. Yet, however disappointing at the time, it was during the Second Vatican Council called by John himself that the question was reopened with a new enthusiasm. There were, now, a number of indications why the whole concept of the worker-priests should be more favourably received. Political contamination was now for some reason less feared, Paul VI, John's papal successor, was more determined in the view that workers would not come to the priests if priests did not first go to the workers, and in addition the Curia in Rome was beginning to realize that bishops might well understand local problems better than someone several hundred kilometres away; as Henri Fesquet writing in *Le Monde* remarked, what did an Italian cardinal who had never been to France know about the mind of a Renault factory worker near Paris? Such a view is to some extent clearly an oversimplified one, but it does single out the crucial issue of the whole experiment and one that was largely met by the new conditions imposed on the worker-priests, or 'prêtres au travail' as they were now to be called.

In 1965 the second phase of the worker-priest experiment

was revived for a trial period of three years. In addition to the change in name, which some argued was too fine a distinction to be generally recognized, there were five important modifications. No priest would be allowed to assume union or other responsibilities during his years of office, though he could become a member of a trade union; there should be a more thorough training before the position was actually taken; the priest should remember that he is and must remain 'un homme d'église'; he should not be isolated but remain in contact with other ecclesiastical bodies in his parish — an idea already practised by the *Mission de France* teams; and as a body the worker-priests should come under the jurisdiction of an episcopal committee headed by the Archbishop of Paris. It is to be seen that the two major differences, therefore, were the attempts to limit the priests' political activities and also to create some kind of organic missionary unit, of which the worker-priest would be a single (albeit the most important) element.

For the most part these reforms were greeted with enthusiasm, though there was some criticism from the ever present traditional and conservative right-wing Catholics who remained in opposition to the whole action of missionary work expressed in these terms, from the few worker-priests who had chosen to disobey their superiors in 1953-4, and from those priests who had continued in 1954 as 'prêtres de la mission ouvrière', some of whom now considered that they and their efforts were being overlooked. In spite of such criticism, however, Paul VI saw fit in November 1968 to prolong this second phase of the worker-priest experiment (during which forty-eight priests had been used) for another three years. During this period further reforms were announced: numbers were no longer to be limited and priests could exercise union responsibilities — a directive which appeared to have been left sufficiently vague to enable Rome to intervene if it was felt that political commitment was becoming excessive. The immediate results were impressive enough and by the end of 1971 over 400 worker-priests were active throughout France. At their general assembly held at Easter 1972, however, only 259 priests were present (72 others having declined to attend). Of these 331, 130 were militant members of the CGT and 78 of the CFDT, and it could have been thought, particularly in the light of more revolutionary developments elsewhere within the Church, that such a reduction in numbers was indicative of a growing sense of frustration and disillusion. Yet the experiment contined and the numbers of worker-priests in full- or part-time employment increased. Furthermore in May 1975 Jean Rémond, a priest with the *Mission de France* since 1950, was raised to the rank of bishop. Rémond is still critical of the Church's attitude to society ('Elle vit dans un monde à elle, un monde qui n'est pas réel'), but his appointment, though relatively insignificant in the general context of Catholic Action, does suggest that the whole experiment has a permanence and that it has the blessing of Rome.

Some structural and organizational changes. During this same period from the early 1940s to the present day a number of far-reaching and influential changes have been made in such disparate matters as parish reorganization and the liturgy in an attempt to refashion the image of the Church in the eyes of the modern world. During the inter-war period there had been attempts to popularize certain liturgical texts, together with a number of biblical commentaries and 'lives of Christ'; in 1967 a new catechism written in a language which, it was hoped, would be more suitable for children was brought into use; in 1972 a proposal was made for a new funeral service in which the priest should no longer be obligatory. Since 1972 as well concern has been widely expressed about religious education in schools and about the provision of special courses for adult lay members of the Church. Although they have been opposed by the traditionalists, groups like *Catachèse 80* and school courses put out by the national committee for Catholic education have become established and have been influential in the organization of annual gatherings of young Catholics at Taizé or in the development of non-confessional cultural centres like the one at La Sainte Baume in Provence. The replacement of Latin by French in services including the mass (where it was used for the first time early in 1965) is something which has also gathered pace during the last ten years in particular, though again not without opposition from the traditionalists.

Further important developments to have appeared during

the last twenty or thirty years include the territorial rearrange-
ment of many parishes, the gradual decentralization of certain
administrative and consultative duties, and an examination of
the conditions under which many priests are required to live
and work (though the decision to launch a pension fund was
only taken as recently as 1972). An episcopal assembly
(*L'Assemblée plénière de l'épiscopat français*), effectively the
most powerful body within the French Catholic Church, now
meets every year and is responsible, through its permanent
council and committees, for religious education, revision of
the liturgy, links with lay members of the Church, the
diffusion of the Catholic press and various small magazines
and so on.

The aftermath of the Second Vatican Council

(a) *Towards a religious revolution?* In many ways such
changes as these are relatively superficial, however. Much
more crucial has been the growing unrest among the clergy —
what the late Jean Daniélou described as 'une crise des
vocations sacerdotales' — particularly since the mid-1960s. In
1964, for example, those priests responsible for country
parishes undertook a survey of their position. Like the worker-
priests before them, they felt that their attempts to integrate
themselves with their parishioners were doomed to failure from
the beginning: inadequate training, insufficient opportunity
for integration, and a sense of isolation within the ecclesiastical framework, were all listed as major contributory factors.
As one priest was recorded as having remarked on his relationship with his bishop: 'L'évêque est un personnage qui passe ...
qui ne sait rien de vous, comme vous ne savez rien de lui'. Some
of the objections raised by these priests were examined by the
bishops at their Assembly at Lourdes late in 1966. Other
suggestions for reform, like the proposal that bishops should
retire at the latest at the age of 75, came directly from Rome,
but for many even these were not radical enough. A new wave
of revolution was beginning to sweep through the Catholic
Church.

The events of May 1968 were in many ways as significant for
the French Church as they had been elsewhere. A number of
leading dignitaries supported student demands for reform and

added further weight to the whole idea of the right to question authority. Marty, elected as bishop of Paris in the same year, showed himself to be in favour of democratic decision taking. As he declared on the night of 10 May: 'Les hommes, tous les hommes, doivent pouvoir être présents librement et activement, personellement ou par leurs légitimes représentants, à toutes les instances de décision.' But matters were developing much more quickly than Marty had perhaps imagined.

In November 1968 a letter signed by over a hundred priests and sympathizers belonging to a movement known as *Echanges et Dialogue* appeared. Their demands and proposals, like those of many progressive Catholics before them, though now more strongly expressed, were for priests to become independent of the structure and the constitution of the Church. They wished to alter, radically, the image and the position of the priest in society and maintained that changes made in the past had ignored this fundamental problem. The priest, they argued, should live independently of his order; he should have the right to express himself freely, to participate in political affairs, to marry and to be allowed a voice in the nomination and deployment of new priests.

By January 1969 over 400 priests had joined the movement. In the same month a further statement was issued in which the whole question of authority within the Church was challenged. What they sought, they maintained, was to introduce 'de nouvelles formes de relations entre évêques, prêtres, et laïcs, indispensables à l'annonce du Christ au monde d'aujourd'hui'. In the spring of 1969 the movement was partly responsible for interrupting a service held by Jean Daniélou, showering the congregation with pamphlets released from the roof questioning Daniélou's right to be a bishop: for whom and by whom had he been elected?

Nor surprisingly *Echanges et Dialogue* was received by many bishops with considerable hostility. Some attempts were made to meet the issues raised and in March 1969 the Episcopal Assembly issued in particular a statement arguing the case for celibacy. The movement continued to grow but in December 1974 was formally replaced by *Camarades Chrétiens critiques*, a movement which is openly more political and seeks to overthrow the Church hierarchy: 'Nous refusons une Eglise qui a choisi le savoir, l'avoir et l'ordre établi. Nous refusons un

Credo, une théologie et une morale préfabriqués. Nous refusons une image de Dieu qui renforce la notion du pouvoir. L'important est d'appeler les chrétiens à prendre leur destin en main, à devenir eux-mêmes théologiens, à gérer eux-mêmes leur vie sexuelle' (June 1975).

During its early life, *Echanges et Dialogue* was certainly the dominant and best organized of the revolutionary bodies within the Church. From the early seventies, however, and even in its 'new' form, it has seen a host of smaller but no less influential groups develop alongside. In this period of 'pluralisme inconfortable' as the episcopal Assembly defined it in 1975, we find, for example, *La Vie nouvelle, Témoignage Chrétien, Chrétiens Marxistes révolutionnaires* and the *Communion de Boquen* under its leader Bernard Besret. Some are only moderately political preferring to work instead towards the establishment of oecumenicalism, others are uncompromisingly militant. In July 1974, for example, Huguette Delanne, leader of the JOCF remarked: 'Nous agissons d'abord parce que nous sommes de la classe ouvrière et non parce que nous sommes chrétiens'. Though extreme, her words are not untypical. Individual priests have incurred episcopal wrath on account of their activities, and some (notably at Toulouse in November 1972) have been dismissed for having forsaken their vow of celibacy. In October 1972 in his speech, 'Pour une pratique chrétienne de la politique', Cardinal Marty underlined the need for debate and discussion. But significantly he also stressed the orthodox view that the Church should not allow itself to become a victim of political struggles. The pastoral mission of the Church should remain pre-eminent: 'les pasteurs ont à rappeler que la politique n'est pas le tout de l'homme' and 'le comportement des évêques et des prêtres en matière politique doit toujours être cohérent avec la mission de l'Eglise et leur mission spécifique dans l'Eglise'. Moreover the erasing from the official transcription of the proceedings of the Assembly of certain interventions made by Guy Riobé, the bishop of Orleans, in which he was sharply critical of the training methods through which men entered the priesthood, can have given little encouragement to those who had hoped for a new progressive spirit to emerge. Even by 1975 there were few signs of initiative from the Assembly; merely a general sense of the need for involvement, of 'un devoir d'accompagnement et de confrontation'.

Both sides, if for different reasons, seemed unable to formulate any positive policy and it was not inappropriate therefore that the PCF, aware of the general climate of unrest should have seized the initiative. In words which recalled the famous 'main tendue' by Thorez in the thirties, Marchais in June 1976 appealed to Catholics to join Communists in a struggle against oppression. It is unlikely that this move will hurry the Church into any radical change of attitude; already the argument of non-involvement has been made. By contrast, however, it is distinctly possible that the political element of Catholic Action will find in his approach just the kind of encouragement which could give its hitherto fairly disparate elements a common focus.

(b) *The traditionalist reaction.* Left-wing progressive Catholics have not been alone in voicing their opinions and in some cases in challenging the Vatican head on. Since the early seventies various traditionalist groups which all to some degree or other chose to ignore the second Vatican Council have expressed concern at what they see to be a severe erosion of the Church's authority. The abbé Georges (*Contre Réforme Catholique*) in 1972 accused both the Second Vatican Council and Paul VI of revolutionary activity; the *Alliance Saint-Michel* whose members profess themselves to be 'excédés par la situation révolutionnaire' have interrupted Paris masses chanting Latin; the *Silencieux de l'Eglise*, whose leader Pierre Debray has accused integrist Catholics of living 'en vase clos dans un milieu de Chrétienté qui n'existe plus', have held a number of general assemblies as direct challenges to those of Catholic Action groups.

No one however has undertaken such a sustained vigorous defence of traditional Catholicism as the former archbishop of Dakar and bishop of Tulle, Marcel Lefebvre. A man who admits to having been vitally influenced by Maurras and for whom communism is 'la plus monstrueuse erreur jamais sortie de l'esprit de Satan', Lefebvre has, by his activities, run close to excommunication. In 1974 his book *Un Evêque parle* expressed his feelings unambiguously. Having challenged social and political trends within the Catholic Church since the early sixties, he founded in March 1972 a seminary at Ecône in

Switzerland for the training of priests along traditionalist lines. (From 32 students in 1972 the seminary had grown to 104 in 1974.) His refusals to accept the Pope's ruling led in 1976 to his being forbidden to ordain priests and on 12 July he was officially suspended from his priestly functions — *a divinis* — a step not far short of excommunication. Lefebvre has not accepted these decisions ('il ne faut pas obéir aux lois lorsqu'elles sont mauvaises') and on 20 August officiated at a mass in Lille attended by 6000 people. Subsequent masses at Besançon and Fanjeaux in September were less well attended, but the message of Lefebvre's sermons has remained constant — a refusal to accept what he sees as the neo-modernist and neo-Protestant developments in the Catholic Church, and an appeal for the restoration of authority in all aspects of society, secular and religious alike. Indeed, references made at Lille to Videla's dictatorship in Argentina as an exemplary form of government prompted left-wing opposition to shower Fanjeaux with leaflets accusing him of fascism.

Although polls taken in August and September suggest that Lefebvre has a high following (between 20 per cent and 30 per cent) it is impossible to estimate with any degree of precision what his support would be in the admittedly unlikely event of his being excommunicated. Early in September he had an audience with the Pope in which he requested that the traditionalist experiment should be allowed to continue. Whether this will be granted is uncertain, but it is most unlikely that Paul VI will be successful in persuading the rebellious Lefebvre to abandon his practices completely. As the president of the Episcopal Assembly, Archbishop Etchegaray, has underlined, this dispute is more than one about the use of Latin or the current ritual of the mass; it is about loyalty to the spirit of the Second Vatican Council and, more crucially, to the Pope himself.

Conclusion

In spite of various attempts to give practical expression to the progressive spirit of the Second Vatican Council and in spite too of the inevitable involvement of the Catholic Church in France with issues like abortion, divorce or nuclear warfare, many have felt, especially during the last fifteen years, that progress has not been quick enough. Paul VI's words in 1971 to Cardinal Roy that 'la foi chrétienne se situe au-dessus et parfois à l'opposé des idéologies' expressed not simply a personal view but a philosophy which has since shown little sign of undergoing any radical alteration. Inevitably therefore it has served rather to increase the frustration felt by progressive Catholics than to encourage them to hope for action. Yet as we can see dissatisfaction, for so long almost solely the prerogative of Catholic Action groups, is now albeit for quite different reasons being voiced by a growing number of traditionalists as well. Although by definition conservative and cautious, the Catholic Church is being forced into a situation where a decision will have to be taken. Moreover, it is ironic that its ultimate attitude concerning Lefebvre may, if only by implication, give a clearer indication of official attitudes towards the progressive groups. Whatever the outcome of these debates and controversies, the temper of the age was perfectly caught by the Protestant Bishop of Strasbourg when he remarked in 1976 that all Christians 'se trouvent dans l'engrenage d'une aliénation dont ils n'auront plus la force de se dégager'. Just how such involvement is resolved remains to be seen.

Bibliography

For a general survey of the period covered by this chapter consult:

Latreille, A. and Rémond, R. (eds.), *Histoire du Catholicisme en France*, Vol. III, pp. 487-684. Paris, Spes, 1962.
Mayeur, J.-M. (ed.), *L'Histoire religieuse de la France, XIXe, XXe siècles. Problèmes et méthodes*. Paris, Beauchesne, 1975. Adopts a thematic rather than a chronological approach. Deals with overseas as well as internal issues.

For a more substantial treatment the following books will prove useful:

Dansette, A., *Destin du Catholicisme Français*. Paris, Flammarion, 1957. Detailed survey of the period 1926-56.
Duquesne, J. *Les Catholiques français sous l'occupation*. Paris, Grasset, 1966. A fascinating well-documented account.

Rémond, R., *L'anticléricalisme en France de 1815 à nos jours*. Paris, Fayard, 1976. An introduction in which anticlericalism is discussed from a variety of angles — sociological, cultural, etc. — is followed by a long historical account of the phenomenon in France. Particularly good on the period from the Second Vatican Council to the present.

Other useful books or articles on particular topics or problems include:

Rémond, R., *Les Catholiques, le communisme et les crises 1929-1939*. Paris, Colin, 1960. A well-documented, lively account of such issues as the industrial strikes in the early 1930s, the Italian invasion of Ethiopia, the Spanish Civil War and the 1936 French elections.

Rémond, R. (ed.), *Forces religieuses et attitudes politiques dans la France contemporaine*. Paris, Colin, 1965. Contains some valuable articles on the influence of the Church on political matters. Includes a chapter on the Catholic press.

Solé, R., *Les Chrétiens en France*. Paris, PUF, 1972. In the main a collection of texts relating to all the central problems which confront both the Protestant and Catholic Churches in France today. An interesting discussion in the last chapter on sexuality, love, celibacy, etc.

A useful collection of documents concerning the worker-priests is *The Worker Priests: A Collective Documentation*, translated by Petrie, J.. London, Routledge & Kegan Paul, 1956. Valuable surveys of the influence and position of the Church in France in recent years have been carried out by the *Nouvel Observateur* (No. 106, November 1966, and Nos. 242 and 243, July 1969) and by *Esprit*, October 1967, 'Nouveau monde et Parole de Dieu', and November 1971, 'Réinventer l'Eglise', which deal with both general and specific issues. The role and status of the priest in particular is examined.

7 The press

W.D. Redfern

Introduction

As with the world's press, the crisis of the French press has
become endemic. Falling sales, decreases in advertising
revenue, huge increases in the cost of paper, highly paid yet
often superfluous staffs, are some of the material causes. Yet
there is no shortage of groups or individuals anxious to buy up
or to initiate newspapers.

France comes eighteenth in the world tables for the number
of newspapers sold per 100 people; and consumption is about
half that of Britain. The obvious inference, that French
citizens are less thoroughly informed on public events than
Anglo-Saxons is tempting but, despite such statistics,
unproven. Proportionately fewer papers are read today in
France than before 1939. The Paris dailies are essentially a
press for the Ile-de-France area. Before the war they sold twice
as many copies as the provincial press, but now sell only half as
many. This exchange of positions started in 1945, when the
metropolitan press was too poorly equipped to develop
provincial editions. Nowadays the regional dailies can obtain
news as quickly as those in the capital, and are physically and
temperamentally nearer to their readers. They continue to
expand their circulations but, rather surprisingly, more in the
countryside than in the towns. This situation stems from the
multiplicity of editions, each specializing in local, even
parochial, news. At the same time, they have experienced the
same concentration of resources as the Paris press. There is an
increasing tendency for regional papers to form *couplages*
(partial mergers), especially in the fields of advertising,

printing and distribution. The aim is to avoid mutually unprofitable competition, particularly on the boundaries of regions where some overlap occurs. Hence the reciprocal non-aggression pacts. One result is that *Ouest-France* recently became the largest daily in France, overtaking *France-Soir* and *Le Parisien libéré*. In general the strength and independence of the provincial press have impeded so far the creation of huge newspaper chains, like those of Great Britain, the United States, Japan or Germany.

During the summer of 1976, however, there was a loud protest from journalists and political figures of the Opposition when Robert Hersant, a financial manipulator of talent, added control of *France-Soir* to that of *Le Figaro*. This act defied the 1944 edict aimed at thwarting press monopolies. M. Hersant was alleged to have been backed by financial concerns and government schemers anxious to establish a solid conservative front before the 1978 elections. Despite resistance by the journalists he employs, Hersant is well on the way to deserving his title of 'the French Axel Springer': already one in six Frenchmen read one of his publications.

There are fewer French papers, national or regional, than before the war, and those that survive are in the main examples of *la presse industrielle*. Like all industries, it has its victims. *Paris-Jour*, with a circulation of a quarter million, had to close down in 1972, after large-scale sackings had led to strikes and fruitless government intervention. It is heartening, however, that the most reliable French newspaper, *Le Monde*, has made the best progress in circulation and been the only daily to make a regular profit. The press in France nevertheless remains big business, and figures about twentieth in the list of French economic giants. It employs nearly 100,000 people and ensures the livelihood of twice that number. The government helps it by indiscriminate aid of various kinds, which amounts to a form of indirect subsidy. Newspapers are wholly exempted from taxes on turnover and various local taxes. They can start tax-free funds in order to fit themselves out with new equipment or can obtain loans from the state. They enjoy preferential postal, telegraph and telephone rates. Overseas sales are subsidized, in keeping with the official policy of spreading French 'culture' the world over. But the weekly political opinion press is currently threatened with having to pay Value Added Tax, a burden which will cripple some.

In France, unlike Germany, the USA or Britain, there is no appreciable difference in price between 'quality' and 'popular' papers. Until 1967, the selling price of French dailies was fixed by the government. The increase in price that year caused a big drop in sales from which most papers have not yet recovered. A chasm separates the cost price and the selling price, and it can be bridged only by actively encouraging advertisers to buy space; three-quarters of the income of *Le Figaro* for example comes from advertisements. Indeed the pursuit of advertisers is even more fierce than that of readers. Whereas in England it often seems to be in its second childhood, press advertising in France, where the market is less buoyant than in many developed countries, is still in its infancy. Between the two wars, a feudal consortium of the five leading Paris dailies, together with the chief agency, conspired to keep the price of advertising space high and thus to shut out any rivals. This monopoly was eventually broken, but today advertising continues to favour the more flourishing papers and to accelerate the downfall of the less successful ones. It is sometimes argued that a paper well off for advertisers eager to use its columns is freer from any pressure they might try to apply than is an economically weak paper. In addition, it is not really necessary for advertisers to pressurize newspapers, for the interests of both sides are identical : to sell as much as possible. Perhaps collusion is a more apt term.

The press in action

The Popular Front. Unlike Britain, West Germany or Austria, France has no Press Council to act as public watchdog, to reprimand editors for defamation of person or otherwise nefarious conduct. While the pressure that such bodies can exercise is mainly of a moral nature, even scandal rags have at times shown themselves sensitive to such disapproval. Since the law of 1881, the French press has, in theory, enjoyed freedom of opinion and expression (except, as we will see later, in times of war and national crisis — though the definition of crisis is always in the hands of the government). That law of 1881 was a classic liberal document inviting open competition (or jungle warfare). Although the notion of a 'free press' is probably an unattainable ideal, it is conceivable that a press could achieve, if it tried to act as a public service, a measure of responsible freedom. But the emotional value of the notion of 'freedom of the press' has blinded many to its sometimes undesirable consequences. The multitude of papers that were born after 1881 produced very quickly an atmosphere of violent sectarian polemics (as during the Dreyfus Affair), rather than one of balanced debate. This phenomenon has recurred at various critical junctures this century, and rarely so virulently as during the Popular Front.

The unrelenting onslaughts of the extremist right-wing press drove the then Minister of the Interior to suicide. Blum was compelled to pass a law designed to curb the use of the press for such lethal scandal-mongering, but it had little effect. Larger in readership and far more high-pitched vocally (the French call tub-thumping journalists *ténors*; during that period, falsettos might have been a more appropriate term), the right-wing press played a large part in liquidating the Popular Front. In 1936, the press as a whole was heavily politicized: political news and controversies took up most of the daily space. While the press of Left and Right waged war on each other, the *grande presse* (i.e. *Paris-Soir, Le Petit Parisien*) acted as usual in opportunist fashion, always on the lookout for sensational aspects. On the whole, press support for the Popular Front was too mild and too unconstructive. In 1936, most of the French voted Left, but the majority read right-wing or so-called 'impartial' papers.

The press post-war and the Algerian Crisis. Just as the political militants engaged in Resistance work were already manoeuvring for supremacy after the Liberation, so newspapermen were determined after the war to make a clean sweep. A great purge of the collaborationist press was carried out. The avengers confiscated and distributed its equipment, premises and capital; the former clandestine press benefited. There were high hopes (still alive today in some journalistic quarters) of setting up a completely reformed, 'decapitalized' press — that is, one freed from the control of financial interests. Polemics erupted as to whether the essential auxiliaries of the press (the paper industries, distributing organizations and news agencies) should be nationalized, or whether this step would put the press at the mercy of arbitrary government. In fact, because of such hesitation, a considerable part of the old order was able to re-establish itself. The much needed statute of the press was blocked in the National Assembly. In the confusion of post-war France, a large sector of the press pushed out varying forms of propaganda, often anti-communist. Much of it was gutter-journalism. When the editor of *Le Monde* advocated neutralism as the only solution to the Indo-Chinese dilemma, he was derided as a eunuch.

As well as the civil war waged at various points in history between newspapers themselves, on occasion the French government has laid its heavy hand on the press. There is a long tradition in France of governmental confiscation or censorship of 'dangerous' publications, dating back to the suppression of anti-government pamphlets in the seventeenth and eighteenth centuries. In fact, the care taken by authoritarian regimes to muzzle the press indicates its importance, especially in those countries where, as in France, the expression of ideas is valued highly (Karl Marx said, with a sting in the tail: 'La France est le seul pays de l'idée — c'est-à-dire de l'idée qu'elle se fait d'elle-même'). During the Algerian crisis, the government had many reasons for wishing to limit dissent in the communications media. One reason was the hostility of the army officers to what they considered as a 'treason press', which they had already blamed for helping to lose them the Indo-Chinese war, by its critical and therefore 'demoralizing' reports. In addition, the government wanted at first to represent the Algerian rebellion as the handiwork of mere terrorists, and later tried to make out that the end had come when it was nowhere in sight, and that peace could be obtained without negotiating with Algerian nationalists. A strong opposition press would obviously hinder such aims. During the Algerian war therefore, papers and periodicals were seized by the police on over 250 occasions in France. The irony was that few convictions followed these seizures, as open trials would have given too much publicity to the government's dubious right of confiscation. To show its 'impartiality', the government sometimes suppressed both right- and left-wing papers.

The government's various actions did not in fact arrest the spread of information, at least to the educated reading public.

A heavy responsibility lay on the French press, because of the state control over television and radio. In addition, the sole French news agency, the *Agence française de presse*, often withheld cables containing items detrimental to the government or other vested interests. In many such ways, public opinion in the 1950s slowly lost contact with events, despite the efforts by several organs to keep readers informed. *Le Monde, L'Express, France-Observateur, Le Canard enchaîné, L'Humanité* and the Catholic monthly *Esprit*, all made sustained protests, or simply printed factual statements that spoke for themselves, especially on the question of torture. The big-selling dailies told very little. Like the torturers themselves who used jargon to shroud their doings, these papers tended to camouflage the whole issue in euphemisms.

The popular press

Randolph Churchill once said that the popular press provided a meal, in which murder was the hors d'oeuvre, a juicy sex-story the dessert, and a Royal Family anecdote or scandal the main course (*Le Parisien libéré* hinted broadly that on their honeymoon Captain Phillips had, as a result of regal demands on him, 'gorn lame'). The first 'yellow' journal in the world was French. *La Gazette burlesque* (Paris, 1650-65) abounded in reports of scandals, crime and society gossip. *France-Soir* continues and extends this tradition. It has a circulation of around 650,000 (which has slumped from nearly a million a few years ago), and covers most of the day and night with successive editions. It took up where the pre-war *Paris-Soir* (nicknamed *Pourri-Soir*, because of its unscrupulousness) left off. In eight years during the 1930s *Paris-Soir* jumped from sales of 60,000 to 2 million by reason of its masses of photos (thus reducing eye strain and brain fag), an enormous staff of reporters everywhere (thus ensuring widest coverage and frequent scoops), and a calculated exploitation of sensationalism. The stress, now as then, falls on 'human interest' stories, strip cartoons and picture serials; on American-style gossip columns and belligerent opinionating (on non-political topics). *France-Soir* also uses the typically French trick of occasionally employing an academician to act as special envoy or commentator on big events. It is doubtful whether it has ever wielded much political influence (popular papers have been called 'leaders who bring up the rear') but, in its pandering to the lower instincts of its readers, it probably has a stultifying effect on their minds. The French popular press, like that of other countries, tends to melodramatize news by presenting politicians as actors in some exotic drama rather than as functionaries, to trivialize it by anecdotage, to warp it by innuendoes and suppositions. All this so that the reader may have the illusion of living, by proxy, more intensely. Such an escapist press offers collective psychotherapy. René Pucheu has said: 'Le journal est beaucoup moins un moyen d'information qu'un moyen d'incantation, il est à la société technicienne ce que le sorcier est à la religion primitive.'

This is especially true of the Sunday press (*France-Dimanche* and *Ici-Paris*). The French Sabbath is given over to a colossal display of sensationalism, cheap sexual titillation, sport, strip cartoons and sentimental stories (preferably involving royalty or the stars of the entertainment industry). On a rather higher level the weekly *Paris-Match*, with a dwindling circulation of around 600,000 and sometimes considered to be the best picture magazine in Europe, fulfils a not dissimilar function. With its commandos of reporters and photographers always on standby to rush to any big event ('*Match* men move in on a story like locusts. After they're through, there's nothing left for anyone else to reap'), *Paris-Match* maintains an 'apolitical' but essentially anti-communist line. Aiming to attract the greatest number possible, it tries to offend none of them, and consequently works hard at smoothing the rough angles of any item. But photos, its staple produce, can bias reporting more insidiously than words do; the camera can and does lie. *Paris-Match* is losing readers steadily, perhaps because it is in effect a static television screen.

Some leading papers

Le Figaro is a rough equivalent to the British *Daily Telegraph*, and is the traditional organ of the conservative and moderate bourgeoisie. It had the advantage of reappearing as early as August 1944, with the same title as before the war and with much the same staff. It is moreover the oldest Paris daily but, despite its circulation of around 400,000, it is heavily dependent for revenue on advertisements for the Paris property market. Its professed policy is eclecticism. Politically, out of fondness for continuity and non-violent evolution, it tends to support the government. It has been called 'la plus à gauche des journaux de droite, la plus à droite des journaux de gauche'. It is clearly a real centre paper, *le juste milieu*. It is proud of its long tradition of using as contributors established writers and academicians. These 'chroniclers' play elegant variations on the stock themes of the literate bourgeois: elegiacs on the passing of time, and the need to preserve certain values against its ravages. *Le Figaro* was the paper that, in his cork-lined room, Proust relied on in order to keep in touch with the outside world, especially the affairs of high society. It has a preponderance of women readers who, it is ungallantly alleged, enjoy perusing the stylish doodlings of venerable men of letters and the society diary pages. Readers of this paper are unlikely to be extremist, avant-garde or very intellectual. It is mainly an undogmatic paper, which prefers to 'compare and contrast' rather than to plug any specific line. Recently its calm has been shaken. Since its take-over in 1975 by Robert Hersant, there have been many struggles between the owner and the editorial staff, some of whom have resigned in order to affirm what was never a very strong independence.

At the other end of the social spectrum, *L'Humanité* has existed for seventy years and has been the official organ of the French Communist Party for three-quarters of that period. In the 1920s, soon after it became specifically communist, *L'Humanité* was subjected to rough treatment by the government. Several seizures of whole issues were made and contributors imprisoned, for inciting the proletariat to strike for better wages and working conditions, and for denouncing French imperialist exploitation in the colonies. At various times in its career, it has supported the Viet-Cong, the Algerian FLN and the rebels in Cuba. But it wore Stalin-coloured spectacles when reporting on the Hungarian uprising in 1956. It suffers attacks from socialists, moderates, extreme right-wingers and, increasingly, is outflanked on the left by more radical elements. As well as calls to direct action, it also plays more often nowadays the waiting game of political alliances. It has half the number of pages of its rivals and has always had to scratch along financially by means of appeal funds and unpaid assistance from readers. Its Sunday version is more of a colour-supplement and subsidizes the daily by selling more than three times as many copies. The present readership of *L'Humanité* is oldish and circulation drops steadily (around 150,000 in 1975). Recently it featured an advertisement for mink coats (once the stock apparel of capitalists' wives in pre-war cartoons), but it receives only 10 per cent of its revenue from advertising sources. It has its day of public glory once a year, when it organizes a fête attracting hundreds of thousands. There, among the fun-fair and the candy-floss, Marxist dogma can be more easily disguised than in the daily paper. For all its numerous faults, however, by its continued existence and its occasional campaigns, *L'Humanité* does remind the world that a large number of often militant communists live in France, and that the French proletariat is probably more politically conscious than its British counterpart.

With a circulation of around 300,000, *L'Aurore* serves a fairly elderly lower middle-class clientèle. It rather uneasily supports the goals of both small businesses and large firms, for the latter constantly threaten the former with take-overs. Despite in effect representing opposition from the Right, generally from the anti-fiscal Poujadist standpoint, *L'Aurore* is strangely regarded by many as left-wing, because it is anti-Gaullist.

The only true *national* daily is the Catholic evening paper *La Croix*, as, unlike the other Paris dailies, it sells its 140,000 copies mainly in the provinces. Starting in 1883 and up to 1914, it published two versions of the daily (one for the élite and one for the popular audience), in keeping with the Catholic convention of hierarchy. After the Second World War, it was regarded with some suspicion, despite De Gaulle's *Nihil Obstat* and the support of the Christian democrat MRP, because it was rather late in 'scuttling itself' (June 1944!). It fulfils a semi-official role as the vehicle of church opinion. Far from being obsessed, however, with religious matters, *La Croix* devotes more space to foreign news and to economic affairs than, for example, *Le Figaro*. Its crucifix symbol was dropped in 1956 with an ensuing increase in sales of several thousand copies but, in the main, the Catholic press in France remains very much a closed-circuit organization, conceived only for the faithful, though there are millions of such faithful. Its financial independence surpasses that of the commercial press, largely because its distribution system excludes costly middle-men. The pattern is : postal subscriptions (90 per cent of the sales of *La Croix*), unpaid home delivery, or stands set up after Mass. On the other hand, *La Croix* wins little advertising (only 10 per cent of its revenue), for its readership, oldish and relatively well-educated, is socially too undifferentiated. Its losses are made up by other enterprises, e.g. printing, in its group. Ecclesiastical advisers sit on the boards of all Catholic publications, but usually exercise their control only after the journal has been published. There is little need for overt interference by the Church hierarchy when self-censoring already prevails. Since 1968, a whole page in *La Croix* called 'Dialogue' is devoted to readers' letters, which over the years seem to have improved in thoughtfulness and avoid the wasteful jokiness often found in the correspondence columns of the British 'quality' press.

Le Monde is the major serious paper. In shape, it resembles the British *Daily Mirror*, but there the likeness ends. Instead of yelling headlines, the reader sees a rather forbidding mass of small print, broken only by the occasional map or graph. The paper's policy is *faire dense*; and the density of its lay-out is counteracted by the intelligence of its content.

Its title reflects its readership, which is world-wide; one-tenth of its 425,000 readers are non-French. It is the paper of the urban élite: the magistrature, administrative grades, diplomats, the whole *Université* (i.e. *lycée* teachers, students and academics), and top men in industry and commerce. Nevertheless, *Le Monde* is often praised by militant trade unionists for the honesty of its reporting. It has the youngest readership of any major French daily, which might explain what many see as its recent leftwards movement, especially in its very sympathetic coverage of Portugal.

It was born four months after the liberation of Paris, and so was rather late on the scene. Most of the team that got it going belonged to the pre-war *Le Temps*. Its initial line was support for De Gaulle and a plea for overdue reforms to benefit the workers and young people of France. Clearly, *Le Monde* set out to be less conservative than *Le Temps*, but it placed the same emphasis on the arts and on international affairs. From the beginning, the guiding idea was to launch a paper free from all kinds of influence, such as big business and political parties. It was immediately attacked by left-wing journals, who thought that it would continue where *Le Temps* had left off, as a semi-official source of government news. But very quickly *Le Monde* differentiated itself from its forebear. Apart from combating external opponents, the staff at times disagreed among themselves, and *Le Monde* did not try to conceal its internal difficulties. With similar frankness, it decided to publish its accounts regularly, a practice unheard of in the French press, in order to prove that no financial lobbies were influencing its policies. In 1951, some former editorial staff attempted to return in order to change the paper's neutralist line on foreign affairs. The reigning editor, Beuve-Méry, offered his resignation, but received so much support from his staff and from readers that he agreed to remain. This was an important stage in the development of the French press, as it established a precedent whereby editorial staff were enabled to demand more participation in running the newspapers they work on. Above all, it was a notable victory against the widespread hatred of independence and fair play. It is said that the communists are less afraid of their heavily biased antithesis *L'Aurore* than of the more objective *Le Monde*. Beuve-Méry believed unashamedly in certain intellectual and moral values, and was always hostile to the lies, scandal-mongering and muck-raking of so much of the world's press. At the risk of boring his readers, he gave a full-spread treatment to all important documents.

Le Monde has naturally made mistakes. Over Suez, it urged that Nasser should be jumped on heavily. On the Algerian question, its policy shifted from one of supporting the spineless Guy Mollet to that of pleading for negotiation with the rebel nationalists. On the other hand, its apparent indecision on some issues is caused by its attempt to represent conflicting opinions. It acts as a forum for discussions. Of all French journals, the non-kow-towing Catholic monthly *Esprit* is perhaps closest in outlook to *Le Monde*, whose staff sometimes publish articles there. Both stand for moderation, independence, liberalism of a realistic kind, 'révolution par la loi'.

Le Monde has no photos or horoscopes, though the amount of space given to advertising has increased substantially during recent years. Precise and vivid reporting is the house rule. It has agreements with *The Times, La Stampa* and *Die Welt* to interchange articles. It diversifies continuously, with regular supplements on the arts, literature, leisure, education, science and economic affairs. It was run until quite recently by a benevolent despot, in close cooperation with a disciplined team. Beuve-Méry was called the misanthrope of the French press, a cactus, a Cassandra-figure. He was hardly any wealthier than his assistants and had a profound scorn for money. He was not anaemic in his moderation and commanded a caustic and, if need be, crude style. His instructions to his staff were twofold : 'Pas de bourrage de crâne, pas de léchage de cul'. In comparison to British newspapers, *Le Monde* is more reliable than the *Guardian*, less shifty than *The Times*, and far less conservative than the *Daily Telegraph*. Its comprehensive and well-informed coverage of foreign news makes all British papers look very insular indeed. Beuve-Méry obviously relished difficulties, 'like selling a boring, expensive newspaper', as he once said. His pseudonym, Sirius, was reminiscent of the French term denoting remoteness of viewpoint, *le point de vue de Sirius*, and it is true that *Le Monde* often takes itself too humourlessly and regards common reality from too Olympian a vantage. The recent attack on it by an ex-staff reporter who charged it with secret subversiveness provoked a pompously self-righteous rejoinder signed by all the leading members of the team and Beuve-Méry himself. For all its efforts at objectivity, *Le Monde* has never claimed to support the conservative side of the great divide in France, and its recent insertion of political cartoons reveals a readiness to offer on occasion very slanted opinions on current events.

Some weeklies

L'Express and *Le Point*. As no serious or even semi-serious Sunday press exists in France there is a greater market than in Britain for weeklies, which have more time for reflection and a more sifted and glamorous presentation. *L'Express*, with a circulation of over half a million, is an interesting case of a journal starting out with a pronounced conscience and gradually shedding or sophisticating it in tune with changes in the times. It first appeared in 1953, as a weekly supplement of the financial daily *Les Echos* (and despite the growth of its financial press France has still no match for the *Economist* or *The Financial Times*). In 1955-6 it tried to transform itself into a daily and failed, though it currently has plans to try again. In 1964 it changed to the news magazine formula. An editorial that year proclaimed that the era of crusades was over. In the last few years, *L'Express* has revealed a taste for its own peace of mind and the stimulation of its readers' bodies. Like its founding editor, Jean-Jacques Servan-Schreiber, it has generally striven to appear young, vigorous, non-conformist but 'with it', explanatory rather than partisan, and slick. It does very well for advertisers. Its public is composed mainly of *cadres* : the 'technocrat' sector, youngish, well equipped with and avid for more creature comforts. It has been said that *L'Express* aims at 'Americanizing' the Left in France. Certainly its present appearance, a near carbon copy of *Time*, suggests that this may be partly true. It goes in extensively for 're-writing' in the house style, and its articles present a pretty uniform idiom.

Le Point, with half the sales of *L'Express*, was founded in 1972 by several refugees from the latter. It is largely non-oppositional and in effect a replica of *L'Express* in lay-out (intellectual/commercial incest, like hypochondria, is a French national sport). But with its practised policy of simplification, *Le Point* makes a point: too much indeed of the language of the French press is self-consciously inaccessible to the general public.

Le Nouvel Observateur. A much more individualistic production than *L'Express* and selling over half as many copies is *Le Nouvel Observateur*, earlier called *L'Observateur*, then *France-Observateur*. It was founded with the intention of playing in the French press the role once taken by the *New Statesman* in Britain. It has always been firmly anti-colonialist and anti-Gaullist, and has frequently supported the PSU. Nevertheless, it has shown itself unafraid to attack those it once favoured (e.g. Mendès-France), when it finds them compromising their stated beliefs. Like *L'Express*, it lost a good many readers after the end of the exciting Algerian crisis.

Yet in 1964 an editorial stated that, in the face of the Americanization of Europe and the alleged depolitization of the public, *Le Nouvel Observateur* had opted to go against the current, convinced that a sufficiently large body of readers wanted to be informed and guided by a left-wing journal dedicated to the democratic revival of France. This faith has been proved justified, for the paper steadily increases in circulation. After the events of May 1968, it rediscovered its old belligerence and today tends, often to the point of silliness, to look for signs of revolutionary change in every walk of life : education, employment and literature, but also films, motoring and fashion. It boasts a team of highly idiosyncratic writers and a more than average number of tough, intelligent women columnists. Although some firms withdraw copy because of the intransigence of its political stances, it carries a good deal of quality advertising, for its readership includes many well-off liberals. Its clientèle is young (20-45 in the main) and composed principally of *cadres moyens et supérieurs*, students, teachers, the liberal professions and trade union executives. Its rather pompously stated ambition (to remain 'un journal d'opinion, pur et dur') is being largely fulfilled. When it changed its format in 1972, to look more like *L'Express*, it sent a quesionnaire to many political, academic and cultural luminaries, asking them what kind of paper they wanted it to be. Most replied : carry on as before, but avoid the trap of radical chic, *suivisme*.

Le Canard enchaîné. *Le Canard enchaîné* is the leading French satirical journal. It began as a trench news sheet in 1916, dedicated to resisting the government's *bourrage de crâne* of the common soldier and citizen. It sought to unmask all official pronouncements, by lampooning the gaps between policy and practice.

Its title stemmed from the old word *canard*, meaning firstly any printed matter offered for public (especially popular) consumption and, secondly, false news. The only papers that the masses, if literate enough to read them, could afford throughout most of the nineteenth century were *canards*, as the high cost of proper newspapers reserved them for an élite. *Le Canard enchaîné* exploits this tradition towards a more honourable goal : 'the demystification of the man in the street'. Its professed policy is to provide 'a clownish but critical parody of the daily press'. To this end, its lay-out apes that of a normal daily and, though it appears weekly, its team's powers of improvisation ensure that its commentary on the news is always up to the minute. It aims to have the same relationship to the daily press as puppet shows have to the theatre.

Its articles are specifically 'made in France'. It reflects what many Frenchmen like to think of as typical Frenchness : *débrouillardise, bon sens*, occasional *engueulades*. Neither *Punch* nor the *New Yorker* is a real equivalent. *Private Eye* is closer, in its often schoolboyish thumbing of the nose at authority, though the *Canard*'s writers are mostly middle-aged, and their dissidence is less flashily contemporary. The *Canard* receives a heavy mail from readers: letters of support, rockets, snippets for that section of the paper devoted to the howlers and other idiocies of public pronouncements. This close contact of readers and journalists lends the *Canard* the air of a club. It is a club, too, in another sense: its comic tactics range from winking innuendoes to thumping puns ('Ne disiez-vous pas, Monsieur de Gaulle, que les Français étaient des veaux? Ils ont veauté pour vous'). With its circulation of nearly half a million (three-quarters of that in the provinces), it clearly has, by French standards, a wide audience. It is most popular with school and university teachers, students and the less affluent members of the professional classes. Its editorial staff work as a cooperative, taking a share of the profits. Each has freedom of expression, but the chief editor retains the right to excommunicate. One of its leading columnists was once sacked for accepting the *Légion d'honneur*.

Its policy of accepting no advertising, either open or concealed, makes it unique in the French press. The result, however, is a rather grubby and old-fashioned appearance, which is perhaps part of its image as a rebellious old war horse. Its standpoint is that of the *frondeur*, the defender of individual and minority freedoms. Its strong polemical tradition prevents its taking sides easily, and it tends to oppose those in power, whether Right, Left or Centre. In the campaign for the Popular Front, it pulled its weight along with other left-wing journals, but once the new government was installed, it attacked Blum and his cabinet for using kid-glove strategies against their ruthless big business enemies. Its absolute pacifism stopped it from backing intervention in the Spanish Civil War, or from castigating the Munich agreements.

Its satire is not exclusively political. It features a good deal of purely verbal humour and some analysis of cultural trends (it is very rude towards the whole concept of modishness). The tone is frequently that of an embittered but still virulent idealism. It is not an anti-social paper. The ideal is 'constructive anarchism'.

Often the rumours it reports are exclusive and well-informed (possibly leaked by insiders). De Gaulle was a godsend. Easily caricatured, his regal style inspired one *Canard* writer to describe his entourage regularly in terms of the court of Louis XIV, and Gaullist politics were in this way presented as a court entertainment in a France that had reverted to monarchy.

In many ways, *Le Canard enchaîné* is outdated and sentimental (one of its heroes is Victor Hugo), but it undoubtedly reflects a native distrust of politicians and a strong desire on the part of most people to be left in peace by the 'powers that be'. The *Canard* has never been seized. One prime minister, urged to suppress a particularly outspoken issue, retorted that he had no desire to become a national laughing stock. This peculiar kind of immunity goes with its status as an institution. Licensed fools, however, lose some of their bite, and the government can point to the *Canard's* untroubled existence as proof of its own liberalism, though this myth was recently punctured when the *Canard's* offices were found to be bugged. Another drawback: regular readers note the strain behind the *Canard's* attempts to be funny about everything; news items are often milked dry. In this age of hidden persuaders, all the same, *Le Canard enchaîné*, like its cousins the geese on the Capitol in Rome, sounds an appealing alarm at every encroachment on freedom. In 1972 it was central to the publicizing of the scandals which disclosed corruption in high Gaullist circles. Financially, it has the last laugh: the *Canard* is the least lame duck of the French press.

The regional press

In 1972 *Le Nouvel Observateur* published an article calling the regional press 'la presse du silence'. In response, provincial owners and editors protested, too much. Content analyses have in fact shown that regional papers studiously avoid raising important local issues, and concentrate on anodyne news items, like opening ceremonies. 'Pour l'infiniment petit,' said the director of the Bordeaux-based daily *Sud-Ouest*, 'nous sommes irremplaçables.' When provincial papers fail to appear, statistics show that social, economic and cultural life in the catchment area suffers badly, and that attendance at funerals drops markedly. 'La nécrologie constitue la base de la vie d'un journal de province', as a *Sud-Ouest* editor said with a straight face. The regional paper is undoubtedly an agent of interconnection between scattered localities and individuals.

Pressures from all quarters, the commonly expressed but inadequately justified fear of upsetting advertisers, the notorious closeness of provincial community life, these are all reasons why the regional press treads carefully. In its defence it should be stressed that the Paris press lets the provinces down by talking more readily of national or foreign issues than of purely regional ones. The large provincial papers, because of their often monopolistic position, are besides right perhaps in trying to remain politically neutral. There are, however, exceptions to the general rule. *L'Est républicain*, for instance, gave extensive support in 1970 to the candidature at Nancy of Jean-Jacques Servan-Schreiber. And for all its glaring shortcomings of moral cowardice, political conservatism, its care not to ruffle the hair of local bigwigs, the regional press at least talks of what interests its readers. It is helped in this service by its elaborate networks of local correspondents, a luxury the Paris dailies simply cannot afford. Indeed, the provincials win both ways, for a good number of top Parisian journalists contribute articles to the regional press. However, with the introduction of modern techniques, the Paris dailies may soon be able to add local pages to their standard editions and transmit them rapidly to the provinces, thus rivalling the regional press on its own ground. But the situation at present is that Paris papers seem to function mainly in the hothouse atmosphere of the capital, largely divorced from the provincial life led by the majority of Frenchmen.

The parallel press

1968 saw the resurrected phenomenon of the *journal mural* (a means of conveying information, slogans, insults, credos and morale-boosts among the rebels), which to many optimistic observers and participants was the writing on the wall for the old France. The often beautiful posters produced by the students of the Beaux-Arts demanded 'information libre'. Liberty of expression was indeed one of the main freedoms sought and temporarily practised by the insurgents. Since 1968, this new press (called variously: wildcat, parallel, underground, alternative or *gauchiste*) has had a remarkable and turbulent career. It can be roughly divided into four main categories: Trotskyist (*Rouge*), Maoist (*Le Quotidien du peuple*), Marxist/Leninist (*L'Humanité rouge*) and anarchist/individualist (*Charlie-Hebdo, Actuel*). The sudden emergence of such papers and often equally sudden extinction (they have been called 'exploding ephemera') are their facts of life, the second caused both by governmental measures of harassment and by internecine strife amongst the *groupuscules*. The first two categories had at their peak sales averaging 30,000, the fourth 100,000, but many dropped drastically to 10,000 or less.

Their innovation has been principally to give a voice to the previously stifled protest of workers, servicemen, convicts, students, pupils and ethnic or sexual minorities. Readers are encouraged to participate directly via letters, the gathering and transmitting of news, the constitution of dossiers. Revolutionary press agencies have been formed in order to coordinate this mass of material. What were at first mainly militants' news-sheets, badly printed and arid in content, have been gradually transformed into often attractive, exciting and professional products.

Contributors often accept no payment for articles; militants tout copies around. There is, however, a big contrast between nationally distributed papers like *Charlie-Hebdo* and intensely local, even one-man, efforts, which measure their sales in dozens. The newer papers cannot really hope to survive on the occasional scoop, and many suffer the fate of becoming very predictable in their commentaries. Of them all, *Libération*, founded in 1973, is the closest to being successful. It almost balances its budget with a circulation of around 20,000. All staff are paid the same (manual worker's) rate. In January 1976, it revealed the names of CIA agents in Paris, and is in fact pledged to print leaked or purloined official documents (government, management, police, army), but only with the agreement of the provider as to the timeliness of publishing them. It carries no advertising and aims at a policy of open books vis-à-vis its readers. It tries to steer clear of all constituted organizations ('militants de la vie et non d'un parti', as many new journalists see themselves). Its free personal advertising pages furnish a place where likeminded people can seek and find each other. In 1976, *Rouge*, centred on Alain Krivine, became a daily. It tries hard to be a forum not only for Trotskyists but also for the whole extreme Left.

Actuel, highly successful with its sales of 90,000, closed in 1975, not for financial reasons, but probably because it had exhausted its vein. It had grown increasingly parasitic, indulging mainly in parodies of the established press. Other papers become blunter through repetition. Scatology is rampant in the underground press. It sometimes seems that, if the widespread manure could be reprocessed, by some natural organic method, of course, and passed on to the ecological press (e.g. *La Gueule ouverte*), the gardens of communes might flourish. Another of the curiosities of the wildcat press is the fantastic development of strip cartoons in which even the heroes are hideously grotesque (though this may stem from slapdash draughtsmanship). All suffer from the debilitating fact of life that to vie with the established press, you have to emulate its organization: distribution systems, advertising, the hard sell. In fact, a type of short-circuit occurs, by which underground journalists write mainly for the initiated, since those they might convert are beneath contempt. 'Aspirant à réaliser la révolution par le plaisir, elle a souvent du mal à exister pour autre chose que son propre plaisir', as *Le Monde* once said of this new press. In addition to these newspapers proper, and improper, roneotyped sheets continue to serve a necessary function in barracks, factories, schools and universities for those disillusioned by traditional organs, parties or *syndicats*.

The anarchist press answers the needs of those sickened by endless doctrinal dispute, and it has strong links with the

Women's Liberation and Gay Liberation movements. The aim of one such publication is typical of many: 'Considérer chaque individu comme artiste afin d'éliminer l'artiste'. The motivation is often as much cultural or 'counter-cultural' as political. There is much free swapping of articles and photos. Yet, just as no truly national daily exists in France, so no comprehensive paper unites all the variegated elements of the counter-culture, which are, in comparison with Anglo-Saxon youth, still relatively unemancipated.

The whole phenomenon of the parallel press clearly alarms the government, which has sometimes resorted, in what seems like panic, to seizures and trials. Sartre (the 'lightning-conductor' of the new press), by accepting the function of director of, and therefore legal responsibility for, several *gauchiste* papers, has tried repeatedly to prove that justice in France as regards the press has 'deux poids, deux mesures'. After he provoked the authorities to arrest him, the official response was a perfect example of Marcuse's concept of repressive tolerance: 'On n'arrête pas Voltaire'. All in all, however, this alternative press acts as a constant thorn in the fleshy side of the Establishment. But it was Sartre himself who said, soberingly, in 1970: 'Les journaux bourgeois disent plus la vérité que la presse révolutionnaire'.

Depolitization

Like all young media, television is often credited with almost magical powers of influence. Nonetheless, as it and the radio are controlled by the state in France, the temptation to use both as conditioning agents has frequently proved irresistible. De Gaulle's big appearances on the little screen were in keeping with his general attitude towards the Fifth Republic: he could make direct appeals, bypassing all encumbrances such as Parliament. There is, then, all the more need for a vigorous independent press to counterbalance such pressures. It seems likely that the 'audio-visual press' has mainly shock value, and that people wishing to inform themselves properly on current affairs need to turn to the written word for commentary and extended explanation. In short, radio and television do not necessarily kill off the press, but rather stimulate the appetite for a serious press.

The introduction of advertising on French television has hit newspapers, but perhaps not so severely as the decline in 'small ads', due to the general economic situation. Furthermore the monopoly system favours the big papers, and Paris dailies kill each other off more often than they succumb to competition from the television. Television is dangerous, not so much in that it steals advertising and thus weakens the press economically, but more in that, being a monolithic and largely unquestioned institution, it stifles thought.

It is difficult to deny that all forms of public communication in France, and this is where Gaullism has most demoralized the nation, bear witness to the phenomenon of depolitization: public apathy in the face of often crucial political matters. Since 1945, the communist *Ce Soir*, the socialist *Le Populaire*, the liberal *Combat* and the Gaullist *La Nation* have died; there are no extreme right-wing dailies at all, though the satirical weekly *Minute* sells 200,000 copies. It can be argued, of course, that as the style of politics itself changes, so does public interest, but it is hard to distinguish what new forms of political awareness may have appeared. Many people are clearly bored with the increasingly formalized nature of politics in France, and transfer their energies to more private concerns (hence the rapid growth of the specialist press, the 'mini-media', dealing in hobbies). The *apolitisme*, especially of the regional press, leads naturally to conservative stances. And yet 'there is a monarchist way of reporting on road accidents'. Every journal has a slant, and none more so than those that claim to be 'pure' newspapers. In these the manipulation of readers' attitudes is at its most surreptitious. Their style of reporting is often neither neutral enough to be 'information', nor intellectualized enough to be 'opinion'. It is governed by and it promotes *attitudes* (unconscious prejudices, fallacies, stereotypes). It has been claimed that educated Russians are better at decoding *Pravda* than Western thinking people are at reading between the lines of our own 'free' press. In addition to editorial bias, there is the matter of that loaded information, on which newspapers rely so heavily, supplied by press attachés and public relations officers: the whole question of the filtering and packaging of facts.

Proust spoke of 'cet acte abominable et voluptueux qui s'appelle: lire le journal'. Perhaps inevitably, the relationship of many readers with the paper of their choice is narcissistic. They gaze at their own face, hear their own voice, their own desires and fears, suitably embellished and projected back to them. There can be few people who read with the express intention, or even the readiness, to be jolted. Most of us can shut off what we do not wish to hear (conversely, attention, once polarized, can be acute). Few readers have time or patience to collate differing versions of the same news in different papers. As a result, opinions are often refuges, non-opinions. Today the temptation is not to *read* a paper but to 'spectate' it. The pages often resemble supermarkets, the new 'iconosphere'. The eclecticism of the present-day press, offering a bit to everyone, works against the notion of responsibility. The number and the variousness of readers are too great for any one line to be presented. While the weeklies can afford to be rather more committed, because they serve fairly faithful minorities, the daily press as a whole is diversifying its contents; papers and magazines are getting closer together in style and material. Some of the more serious organs like *Le Monde* resist the contemporary craze for built-in obsolescence, by stressing the documentary function of the press (e.g. the publication of annual indexes of articles to facilitate reference back), but this is exceptional.

Sociétés de rédacteurs

Some of the most glaring shortcomings of the French press date back a long way. Over the past twenty years, the most hopeful signs of reform have come from within the journalistic profession itself, in which three warring factions predominate: the owners, the editorial staffs, and the technical operatives. The complexity of agreements and the marked individualism of the parties concerned have impeded the growth of honourable efficiency. The powerful union of printers has imposed high wages and underemployment of staff, by using archaic standards for calculating work loads. Although modern machines have been introduced, profitability has shown little increase, because the same number of men as before work them. In the 1969 troubles at *Le Figaro*, the technicians did not side with the editorial staff in its resistance to the owner's bid for complete control.

Since late 1974, open war has raged on *Le Parisien libéré*, a big-selling popular daily, between the owner Emilien Amaury and the monopolizing printing-workers' union (the *Fédération du Livre* — CGT). There have been broken agreements, sieges of premises, assaults on blackleg personnel, hijacking of pirate editions. The owner and his chief executive, Claude Bellanger, both make great play of their Resistance record, although in this particular confrontation it is hard for outsiders to tell which side is the Maquis and which the repressive occupying force. The owner presents his struggle as a democratic crusade against would-be totalitarian communism and its attempts to control editorial matter, and to dictate the size of the work-force. The only clear results in two years of battling have been the owner's decision to spend large sums in order to construct alternative printing-works and new distribution-systems, and the drop in circulation by one-half. Elsewhere, in July 1976, Paris Newspaper owners, excluding M. Amaury, and printers' unions settled their long dispute over technical modernization (photo-composition and computer typesetting).

A good many journalists refuse to envisage the press as simply a commercial proposition, and are haunted by theories about the corrupting power of money and by romantic visions of a press akin to knight-errantry. For them, papers should offer their readers 'daily refresher courses', an *éducation permanente*. To idealistic journalists, it is as scandalous that industrialists should control papers as it would be to most people if they controlled law courts or universities. And this statement by a powerful press lord, taxed with having sold out to big business interests, unwittingly illustrates what they are reacting against: 'Je ne me suis jamais vendu qu'à mes lecteurs'. The spokesmen for reform realize that the opponents of any proposed *co-gestion* in producing papers will raise the old alarmist bogyman of 'des soviets partout!' Few reforms are as radical as this. Some would settle for American-style foundations, which would run papers as limited-profit companies. The *sociétés de rédacteurs* that have already been set up on *Le Monde* (in which the editorial staff hold shares), *Le Figaro* and *Ouest-France* see themselves as active watchdogs, ensuring that news is not treated purely as a commercial product and that editorial staff have a real say in all decision-making.

The common belief of such *sociétés* is that the press faces the same problems as society at large: in particular, the need to democratize the remaining autocratic structures. They recognize that part of their programme must include a better training for journalists themselves; and university degree courses have been established at Paris, Lille, Strasbourg and Bordeaux. Refresher courses, especially in economics, about which many journalists are as under-informed as the general public, have also been laid on. In this whole area of reform, the French pressmen have outstripped their British colleagues, who have only recently begun actively to question the present functioning of the mass media and to propose needed changes.

One recent proposal made in *Esprit* is that *sociétés de lecteurs*, akin to consumer-protection groups, are at least as necessary as those of journalists. There is clearly a need for 'informational militants': self-appointed journalists who cross-check reports from news agencies or who raise hushed up and forgotten issues. The biggest need is for plurality of viewpoints, though even pluralism should have its limits. Why, for instance, weep over the material difficulties of badly conceived and ill-run rags?

Conclusion

Edmund Burke spoke of the press as the Fourth Estate, alongside the judiciary, executive and legislative powers. What kind of a force is the French press? It has been suggested that, like that of the Latin nations in general, it is more of a 'tribune' press, which goes *to* the people instead of coming from it, or at least conversing with it. Hence the large amount of pontificating, the paternalism and the lack of attention given to readers' letters (which could act as a feed-back and the start of a dialogue), in most journals. One explanation, among many others, for the depolitization of the French press is the inhibiting historical example of *Le Petit Journal*. At the time of the Dreyfus Affair, it had the widest circulation of all French papers. But it campaigned for Dreyfus; it lost half its readers. Consequently, there is a widespread reluctance to meddle or to shock, at least openly, for all papers try indirectly to direct opinion, by veiled allusions, undocumented sources, omissions or by effects of juxtaposition. Comment disguised as news is a constant ploy.

Perhaps the two features of the French press that most strike a foreign reader are, firstly, the *médisance*, the personal bitchiness, the bristly sense of 'honour' common to French journalists of all persuasions; this derives in part from the importance granted to ideas, to ideologies. Secondly, there is the impression that French journalists, even mediocre ones, are soaked in history, politics and literature. Occasionally, this cultural formation proves too facile, turns to *déformation professionnelle*, and produces (like French lawyers, and like many of the readers who write to their papers) a kind of cheap sub-literature, replete with rhetorical effects. Just as there is a long tradition of sedentary anthropology in France, so there is one of armchair journalism, which relies too much on printed sources or imagination and too little on going to look for oneself. Perhaps a better result is that, in *L'Humanité*, addressed among others to manual workers, can be found long words and cultural allusions beyond the imaginings of the British popular press. Even *France-Soir* publishes occasional serious articles. A lack of matter-of-factness can be a handicap but also a blessing.

Prophets see both the press and books as moribund industries. It might be that papers will fairly soon become a privilege for the well-off minority, as they started out by being, because costs in future will be more closely matched by much increased selling prices. *Paris-Jour*, in that it had most blue-collar workers in its readership, was the most 'popular' paper in Paris before it died in 1972. After it closed, it seems that its readers did not switch to any other paper. It is sometimes said that Paris has room for only two morning and two evening papers. The sad part of the success of *Le Monde*, over which it would be intellectural snobbery to rejoice too much, is that readers at the bottom end of the earning scale might eventually be deprived of what is in many cases their sole source of reading matter. It is yet another indication of the separate orbits in France of the intelligentsia and the masses. René Pucheu offers a salutary reminder that 'la bêtise n'est pas un privilège des non privilégiés'.

Bibliography

Albert, P., *La Presse*. Paris, PUF, 1968. A general study, short but accurate.

Bellanger, C. (ed.), *Histoire générale de la presse français*, 5 vols. Paris, PUF, 1969-76.

Bercoff, A., *L'Autre France: l'underpresse*. Paris, Stock, 1975.

Cayrol, R., *La Presse écrite et audiovisuelle*. Paris, PUF, 1973.

Derieux, E. and Texier, J.C., *La Presse quotidienne français*. Paris, Colin, 1974.

Manevy, R., *La Presse de la IIIe République*. Paris, Foret, 1955.

Pucheu, R., *Le Journal, les mythes et les hommes*. Paris, Editions Ouvrières, 1962.

Schwoebel, J., *La Presse, le pouvoir et l'argent*. Paris, Seuil, 1968. Good on the *sociétés de rédacteurs*.

Varin d'Ainville, M., *La Presse en France*. Paris, PUF, 1965.

Voyenne, B., *La Presse dans la société contemporaine*. Paris, Colin, 1962. Updated regularly. The best general study; fully documented.

The 'Kiosque' series published by Colin contain several fascinating studies of the press in action in the context of contemporary history: e.g. *La Gauche hebdomadaire, La Presse clandestine, Le Monde et ses lecteurs, Le Cas Paris-Soir*.

The monthly *Presse-Actualité* is a goldmine of up-to-date information. The February 1971 number of *Esprit* is devoted to the French press. It contains articles on *Le Canard enchaîné, Le Monde* and *Paris-Match*, as well as discussions of advertising, the financial situation of the press, etc. The March 1972 issue has an excellent article on the parallel press. *Le Monde* has a column on the press at least once every week.

Contributors

JOHN FLOWER, M.A., Ph.D., Professor of French, University of Exeter. Main interests — French literature and history of ideas, literature and politics from the late nineteenth century to the present day. Publications include *Intention and Achivement: an essay on the novels of Francois Mauriac* (Oxford University Press), *Georges Bernanos: 'Journal d'un curé de campagne'* (Arnold), *Roger Vailland, the Man and his Masks* (Hodder & Stoughton). Editor of the *Journal of European Studies*.

ANDRÉE SHEPHERD, L.ès L., Agrégée d'Anglais, Lecturer in English, University of Tours. Main interests: twentieth-century French and English sociology and politics. Publications include a study of the occupation of French factories in May 1968, *Imagination in Power* (Spokesman Books), a translation of Serge Mallet's book *The New Working Class* (Spokesman Books), and contributions to the *Encyclopédie de civilisation britannique* (Larousse) and *Littérature anglaise* (Bordas). Research in progress on the New Left in Britain.

ERIC CAHM, B.A., Head of the School of Languages and Area Studies, Portsmouth Polytechnic. Main interest — the history of French political thought and the French parties, especially of socialism and nationalism. Publications include *Politics and Society in Contemporary France 1789-1971: a documentary history* (Harrap), *Péguy et le nationalisme francais* (Amitié Charles Péguy) and articles in French journals on Péguy and Jaurès.

MALCOLM ANDERSON, M.A., D.Phil., Professor of Politics, University of Warwick. He has published *Government in France: an Introduction to the Executive Power* (Pergamon), *Conservative Politics in France* (Allen & Unwin), and various articles on France. He is also general editor of the series Studies in Political Science, for Allen & Unwin.

ALAN CLARK, B.A. Ph.D., Senior Lecturer in French, University of Canterbury, Christchurch, New Zealand. Main interests — French literature, intellectual, social and political history since 1870. Publications include a number of articles on the fiction and ideas of Bernanos and a short monograph on social development in France since 1944.

MARGARET SCOTFORD ARCHER, B.Sc. (Econ), Ph.D., Reader in Sociology, University of Warwick. Main interests — the development and change of educational systems, European social structure, and macro-sociological theory. Publications include *Social Conflict and Educational Change in England and France: 1789-1848* (Cambridge University Press), *Students, University and Society* (Heinemann) and *Contemporary Europe: Class, Status and Power*, edited with S. Giner (Weidenfeld & Nicolson).

WALTER REDFERN, M.A., Ph.D., Reader in French Studies, University of Reading. Main interests — French literature and in particular the novel from the eighteenth century to the present day. Publications include *The Private World of Jean Giono* (Blackwell), and *Paul Nizan: Committed Literature in a Conspiratorial World* (Princeton University Press).

Index

As in previous editions this index contains only selected references to names, titles, events and institutions of particular importance.